the 50
GREATEST
CHURCHES AND
CATHEDRALS
OF GREAT BRITAIN

IN ASSOCIATION WITH
TIMPSON

the 50 GREATEST CHURCHES AND CATHEDRALS OF GREAT BRITAIN

SUE DOBSON

Published in the UK in 2019 by
Icon Books Ltd, Omnibus Business Centre,
39–41 North Road, London N7 9DP
email: info@iconbooks.com
www.iconbooks.com

Sold in the UK, Europe and Asia
by Faber & Faber Ltd, Bloomsbury House,
74–77 Great Russell Street,
London WC1B 3DA or their agents

Distributed in the UK, Europe and Asia
by Grantham Book Services, Trent Road,
Grantham NG31 7XQ

Distributed in Australia and New Zealand
by Allen & Unwin Pty Ltd,
PO Box 8500, 83 Alexander Street,
Crows Nest, NSW 2065

Distributed in South Africa by
Jonathan Ball, Office B4, The District,
41 Sir Lowry Road, Woodstock 7925

Distributed in India by Penguin Books India,
7th Floor, Infinity Tower – C, DLF Cyber City,
Gurgaon 122002, Haryana

Distributed in Canada by Publishers Group Canada,
76 Stafford Street, Unit 300, Toronto, Ontario M6J 2S1

Distributed in the USA by Publishers Group West,
1700 Fourth Street, Berkeley, CA 94710

ISBN: 9781-78578-487-3

Images – see individual pictures

Typeset and designed by Simmons Pugh

Printed and bound in Great Britain by Clays Ltd, Elcograf S.p.A.

ABOUT THE AUTHOR

Sue Dobson is an award-winning travel writer and magazine editor with a passion for discovering the world, its art, music, religions and cultures. A lifetime of travelling has taken her through all seven continents and her work is published in guidebooks, magazines and online. Home is a pretty village in the English countryside, but she's never happier than when out exploring – churches and cathedrals being high on her list of 'must-sees'. She is a member of the British Guild of Travel Writers and a Fellow of the Royal Geographical Society.

CONTENTS

INTRODUCTION

Towering over the landscape, masterpieces of art and architecture, churches and cathedrals are among the finest buildings in Britain. Vibrant places of worship, they provide a unique record of the nation's history and heritage. Many can trace their beginnings to Anglo-Saxon times and millions of us visit them every year.

In a show of power after the Conquest of 1066, the Normans set about constructing castles and building or rebuilding abbeys and cathedrals in strategic locations in England. Built in the Romanesque style from northern France, they were breathtaking technical achievements, vast in size and featuring massive columns and rounded, semi-circular arches to support the weight of heavy roofs. The great piers that line the nave at Durham Cathedral are always one of the abiding memories its visitors take home.

Then during the 12th century a new style emerged, again from northern France, with sophisticated techniques that would reduce the weight on walls via pointed arches, ribbed vaults and flying buttresses, allowing for more window space and opening up a raft of technical and engineering possibilities.

This Gothic incarnation would be developed down the centuries as architects and masons created ever-more daring and complex designs. Buildings rose to dizzying heights and decoration became more and more detailed and ornate.

As cathedrals were built over lengthy periods, their construction often halted by fire or plague (or both), not to mention collapsing towers, so new styles were incorporated as fashions in architecture changed. The emphasis was always on height and light, often through windows filled with stained glass that brought Bible stories to life for the first time. With their walls covered in frescoes and statues brightly painted, they would have been filled with colour and life.

Salisbury Cathedral is unique in that it was built in one style, Early English Gothic, over a period of just 38 years from 1220. When window tracery became more complicated and decoration richer, this evolved into what became known as Decorated Gothic style, Exeter Cathedral being a prime example.

Perpendicular Gothic followed and was unique to England. Arches were flattened, huge windows inserted in slimmer walls, ceilings became a maze of ribs but most spectacular of all was the fan vaulting, seen in all its breathtaking glory in Gloucester Cathedral's cloisters and in the ceilings of King's College Chapel, Cambridge and Christ Church Cathedral, Oxford.

Then came King Henry VIII's break with Rome and the Reformation. There were an estimated 1,000 abbeys in England and Wales during the Middle Ages and Henry's Dissolution of the Monasteries closed most of them. Stripped of their valuables they were plundered for their stone.

The ruins of some of the great abbey churches remain as monuments of national importance, such as at Glastonbury, Whitby and Tintern. Others survived to become parish churches and continue their role among the communities that bought them, for example Tewkesbury, Romsey and Sherborne. The King saved a few by establishing new dioceses and refounding their monastic abbeys as cathedrals – think Peterborough, Gloucester and Bristol.

While the effects of the Reformation intensified under King Edward VI and his archbishop Thomas Cranmer, worse was to come. With the English Civil War came an era of destruction and desecration by the iconoclasts. Yet somehow these buildings survived to rise again, stumbling badly along the way, and it was essentially thanks to the Victorians in the 19th century that we have the great cathedrals we see today.

One name that appears time and again throughout this book is Sir George Gilbert Scott (1811–78). A keen interpreter of the Gothic Revival style of architecture, he worked on nearly 200 churches, abbeys and cathedrals, either building or restoring them. On his death, his son John Oldrid Scott took up the baton. Despite his prodigious work on ecclesiastical buildings, he is probably best known as the architect of the Albert Memorial in Hyde Park and the St Pancras Renaissance Hotel.

With the formation of new Anglican dioceses in the late-19th and early 20th centuries, a new cathedral for Cornwall was built in Truro and several former parish churches became cathedrals, among them Chelmsford and St Edmundsbury.

Ancient cathedrals and churches can tell a story but so, too, can modern buildings, albeit rather different. Guildford Cathedral's post-war 'Buy-A-Brick' campaign is remembered by families throughout the land and despite the tortuous evolution of Liverpool's much-decried Catholic cathedral, it is now a firm local favourite and high on the 'must-see' list for thousands of tourists enjoying the revitalised city.

What makes a Christian church a cathedral has nothing to do with size. Situated at the heart of a diocese, a cathedral is a bishop's church. It is the site of the bishop's chair (*cathedra*, from the Latin for chair) or throne, symbol of the bishop's (or in some cases archbishop's) ecclesiastical and spiritual authority.

Cathedrals and churches are treasure houses of art and history, testimony to the skills of engineers and mathematicians, stonemasons and sculptors, carpenters and woodcarvers, fresco painters and stained-glass artists down the centuries. So they remain today, as talented craftspeople work quietly behind the scenes, conserving, repairing and restoring the fabric.

They are also the source of wonderful music, their choirs often world-renowned. The Three Choirs Festival, alternating between the cathedrals of Worcester, Gloucester and Hereford, is one of the highlights of the musical year.

Although they are a window on the past they are also very much of the 'now' and constantly look to the future, always conscious of their role as a place of worship and care for the community. The new millennium has seen many a parish church fundraising to install access for all, toilets and a kitchen, while reordering space to make it more flexible.

Major projects at cathedrals include visitor information and welcome centres, good cafés and restaurants, meeting rooms, conference and educational centres, with their naves and chapels often providing the setting for talks, concerts, dinners and events. Some new building developments, as at Norwich and Southwark Cathedrals, have won awards for their architecture.

New works of art and stained-glass windows by contemporary artists and sculptors have been, and continue to be, commissioned. The spectacular 'living water' font at Salisbury Cathedral, the stunning corona over the altar in Hereford's cathedral and John Piper's brilliant tapestries at Chichester are truly memorable. The ongoing decoration of Westminster Cathedral means it displays some of the very finest contemporary ecclesiastical art and craftsmanship.

Standing 'at the still point of the turning world' churches and cathedrals are places where, in beautiful, awe-inspiring surroundings, tourists, pilgrims and locals alike can find spiritual refreshment. I hope the following pages will inspire you to visit and to make discoveries of your own.

BATH ABBEY

At the heart of the city's busy shopping streets, in a piazza of cafés and milling crowds, Bath's magnificent Abbey Church of Saint Peter and Saint Paul presents a story in stone like no other. Its unique west front has angels clambering up ladders (and occasionally slipping down a rung or two) alongside columns of supporting saints and Christ sitting in Majesty between turrets at the top. A statue of King Henry VII watches over the door.

So great is the sense of beauty and unity of the architecture within, that it comes as a surprise to discover that the Abbey's nave and aisles are actually Victorian, albeit a replica of Tudor design. The glorious fan vaulting that carries the eye the full length of the church seems all of a piece, but only the chancel vault originates from the 16th century.

The story of the Abbey goes back into the mists of time – there was even a site of worship here in pre-Christian times. Although little is known about the Benedictine Anglo-Saxon abbey, it is recorded that King Edgar the Peaceful was crowned in Bath in 973.

The form of that service, devised by St Dunstan, the then Archbishop of Canterbury, has formed the basis of all coronation services down the centuries, including that of Queen Elizabeth II in 1953. This pivotal moment in history is commemorated in the Edgar Window at the end of the north aisle.

The Norman conquerors began an extensive building programme in the early 1090s. The bishopric had been at

Photo: Granboca

nearby Wells in 1088 when John of Tours was made Bishop of Wells. A few years later he was granted the city of Bath, the abbey and monastic buildings, and promptly set grand plans into motion.

Not only would the bishopric be moved to Bath, he would extend the monastery, build a bishop's palace and replace the Saxon abbey with a massive new cathedral. After his death, the work continued under Bishop Robert of Lewes, with the cathedral completed in the 1160s. It was so vast that today's Abbey would fit into its nave.

Bath's importance declined when the bishops made Wells their principal seat of residence during the 13th century. The monks found the upkeep of the buildings difficult and by the time of the Black Death in 1398, which decimated their numbers, it had become impossible. The great cathedral descended into decay.

When Oliver King, Bishop of Bath and Wells, arrived in 1495, tradition tells that he had a dream in which he saw angels ascending and descending ladders to heaven and heard a voice telling him to build a new church. This has since been dismissed as a marketing myth, conjured by a desperate fundraiser a century after Bishop King's death, but building began and the angels keep their secrets on the west front.

The bishop commissioned King Henry VII's finest master masons, Robert and William Vertue, to build in the Perpendicular Gothic style. They promised him 'the finest vault in England' (and went on to work at Westminster Abbey). The building was in use but not completed when Prior Holloway and fourteen monks surrendered it to King Henry VIII in 1539.

Looted, the stained glass ripped out and destroyed, the lead stripped from its roof, the shell was sold on to local gentry. In 1572 it was presented to the City Corporation and citizens of Bath for use as their parish church. The nave was given a simple roof and the east end used for services. Houses soon surrounded it and the north aisle became a public passageway.

By the early 19th century Bath Abbey was again in dire straits. Three restorations took place under the city architect but it was Charles Kemble, appointed Rector in 1859, who really came to the rescue.

He commissioned the noted Gothic Revival architect Sir George Gilbert Scott to draw up plans for a complete restoration – and funded much of it himself. Work began in 1864 and transformed the interior, resulting in the awe-inspiring church we see today.

Scott looked to Bishop King's vision and the work of the Tudor master masons, so meticulously matching the design of their fan vaulting in his nave that you have to look very carefully to see the joins. When the Abbey reopened in 1871, Scott felt he had completed the building as the medieval craftsmen had intended.

Pointed arches and flying buttresses enabled the late Perpendicular builders to maximise window areas. In Bath Abbey they occupy some 80 per cent of the wall space and the Victorian stained-glass artists and glaziers filled them well.

The great east window, which depicts 56 events in the life of Christ, from the Annunciation to the Ascension, rises to the full height of the wall and contains 818 square feet (76 square metres) of glass. Partially destroyed by air raids in 1942, it was repaired by the great grandson of the original designer.

The great west window – known as a Pentateuch Window because it tells of stories and events from the first five books of the Bible – ascends in three tiers, from the creation of Eve up to the Passover when the Israelites were delivered from slavery in Egypt.

The nave and quire aisles are lined with memorial tablets – 641 of them, only Westminster Abbey has more – and on the floors are 891 grave slabs (ledger stones) dating from 1625 to 1845. As well as recording the name and dates of the person buried there, many of these contain interesting inscriptions about the person, their family and their life in the local community.

Abbey benefactors get their place in the limelight, none more so than John Montague, Bishop of Bath and Wells in 1608, who donated a tidy sum for the nave to be roofed after the king's commissioners had left it open to the elements. His effigy-topped table tomb is grandly placed behind iron railings between the north aisle and the nave.

In the 18th century, the north transept was where the city housed a fire engine. Now it is home to the renowned Klais Organ, installed in 1997. The delightful frieze of twelve angel musicians, carved in lime wood, was added above the quire screens ten years later.

Do take a closer look. Each angel has its own definite character and the designer, sculptor Paul Fletcher, had a sense of humour. Two violinists face each other as if playing a duet, one using her wings to shield her ears from the bagpipes next to her. Only the cellist is looking towards the conductor, and she has her eyes closed.

The 20th century saw restoration and additions and now Footprint, an ambitious £19.3 million building programme started in 2018, has been designed to bring the Abbey firmly into the 21st century.

Crucially it involves the repairing and stabilising of the floor, which is collapsing, and installing an eco-friendly heating system that utilises the energy from Bath's famous hot springs. By building underground it opens up new spaces to provide such important facilities as toilets, a café and meeting rooms. There'll also be a purpose-built Song School and a Discovery Centre to tell the Abbey's story. As for the completion date, that's likely to be 2021 at the earliest.

BEVERLEY MINSTER

From its sheer size and impressive architecture – it's said that its beautiful west front was the model for that of Westminster Abbey – you could be forgiven for thinking that Beverley Minster is a cathedral. It is larger than many English cathedrals (and more impressive than some) but in fact it is a parish church, one of three in this busy market town in the East Riding of Yorkshire. Its title of Minster goes back to its foundation as an important Anglo-Saxon missionary teaching church, from where the canons went out to preach among neighbouring parishes.

It is hard to imagine that such a magnificent building was destined for destruction in 1548 during King Henry VIII's dissolution of the monasteries. Thankfully a group of the town's wealthy businessmen bought the Collegiate Church of St John the Evangelist for its continued parochial use. Best known today as Beverley Minster, it is the Parish Church of St John and St Martin.

Beverley is often compared with its bigger sister, York Minster (page 258). They were built around the same time, from creamy white limestone quarried near Tadcaster and probably by the same masons. Less imposing it may be, but Beverley has an elegance and beauty all of its own.

Photo: Michael D Beckwith

Its twin west towers soaring skywards, the exterior of the building with its flying buttresses and arcading, statues set in canopied niches and the elaborate tracery of its windows, all hint at the glories to be discovered within.

The Minster owes its existence to St John of Beverley, who died in 721 and was canonised in 1037. Today his remains lie in a vault beneath the nave. A renowned preacher and evangelist, John was Bishop of York when he founded a monastery to retire to in what was then a remote, uninhabited spot. The town of Beverley grew up around it and thrived.

Miracles were attributed to him, ensuring a constant flow of pilgrims to his tomb and shrine. King Athelstan, grandson of Alfred the Great, credited John of Beverley with his victory at the decisive Battle of Brunanburh in 937. In thanksgiving he granted the Saxon church important rights and privileges and established a college of canons. When King Henry V triumphed at the Battle of Agincourt in 1415, he attributed his success to St John and made him one of the patron saints of the royal family.

This is the third church on the site (little remains of its Saxon and Norman predecessors). Construction began in 1190 and continued for the next two centuries, its architecture encompassing the three main Gothic styles: Early English, Decorated and Perpendicular.

You enter through the door of the Highgate Porch, its carved triangular portico watched over by the seated Christ flanked by the twelve Apostles. Light floods the long nave, a vista of white limestone and polished Purbeck Marble, elegant arches, complex arcading and, stretching the full length of the Minster, a pale stone vault with painted tracery highlighting the gilded stone bosses.

Look back to the great west window, depicting the story of Christianity in the north of England, and below it, the magnificent west doorway. Tiers of stone statues under delicate canopies flank the flowing lines of a finely carved ogee arch, crowned by the figure of St John of Beverley. The carvings on the oak doors are of the Four Evangelists and their symbols, created, like the extraordinary canopy that tops the Norman font, in 1728 by the Thornton family of York.

Ahead, the high altar can be seen framed by the central arch of the oak screen that separates the nave from the chancel. Richly carved with saints, bishops and musical connotations, it supports the fine organ, its casing equally ornate, its pipes splendidly coloured.

In the medieval period, Beverley was the centre of secular music in the north of England. The Minster's collection of over 70 medieval musician carvings in stone and wood, believed to be the largest in the world, has been the source of much of our knowledge of early musical instruments.

Many are at the base of the arches in the north aisle and atop pillars in the nave, but they are dotted all around the building as if tempting the visitor to seek them out. They show about twenty different instruments, including bagpipes, fiddles, trumpets, flutes, pipes, shawms and cymbals.

The quire and its early 16th-century carved wood quire stalls are one of Beverley Minster's great glories. In the back row, tall canopies soar into a forest of pinnacles and crocketed spires while kings, saints and bishops stand proud above a lacy woodland of foliage and faces.

The ends of the stalls are carved with strange creatures and poppyheads, and beneath the seats is the largest set of misericords in any church in the country, 68 in all. Under each ledge that supported weary monks during long services, whole scenes of medieval life are portrayed in fine detail and often with a sense of humour or irony.

Originally built in around 1340 the quire has had a tortuous history. Mutilated and defaced, plastered over, hidden, then restored and rebuilt in 1826, like a picture gallery its niches are filled with mosaics of the twelve Apostles and saints, flanked at the base by stone figures associated with the life of St John of Beverley. A winding staircase leads to a platform at the top of the reredos where the saint's shrine, richly embellished in gold and silver, was placed, centre stage for all to see.

The unusual *trompe l'oeil* floor of the quire, laid in the 18th century, gives the illusion of raised stepping-stones. It leads the eye to the high altar and behind it, the magnificent stone-carved reredos.

Alongside the altar is a plain, polished stone sanctuary chair, or frith stool, that dates from the earliest days of the Saxon monastery and is one of only two still in existence. The right of sanctuary for fugitives, given to the town of Beverley by King Athelstan, was abolished under King Henry VIII.

Adjacent to the high altar in the north quire aisle, the exquisitely carved 14th-century canopy of the Percy tomb is considered the jewel in Beverley's not inconsiderable crown. The Percys were one of the richest and most powerful families in the north and the tomb is believed to be that of Lady Eleanor Percy who died in 1328.

A masterpiece of the stone carvers' art – five master masons are said to have worked on it – it rises majestically in a flurry of figures, fruit and foliage. At the pinnacle on the north side, angels bearing the instruments of the Passion attend the risen Christ; on the south side, Christ receives the soul of the dead person into heaven. The whole canopy, a medieval view of paradise, somehow survived the Reformation and the Civil War and remains remarkably intact.

Also in the north aisle, the well-worn steps of a double

staircase once led up to the chapter house, used by the college of canons. It was demolished when no longer required after the dissolution of the monastery, the stone sold to fund the purchase and preservation of the Minster.

The east window contains most of the medieval glass that survived the Reformation. It watches over the retroquire where pilgrims would have passed to get as close as possible to St John's shrine. Look for the superb vaulting and splendid use of Purbeck Marble in the fine arcading. A single lancet window and accompanying copper sculptures, designed in 2004 by Helen Whittaker and known as the Pilgrim Window, have created a space for meditation and prayer.

That the Minster is so magnificent today owes much to two periods of restoration. In the early 18th century the church, neglected and decaying, was listing badly, with the north transept wall leaning four feet out into the street. Advice on how to save it was sought from the renowned architect Nicholas Hawksmoor, best known for his work with Christopher Wren and John Vanbrugh, and as the designer of six London churches.

An ingenious way of righting the structure was devised. Using a wooden cradle, ropes and pulleys, over eleven days the entire wall was pulled back upright. Although many of Hawksmoor's additions and renovations were removed during the 19th century, the fine stone floor in the nave and his dazzling geometric marble pavement in the chancel remain, as does the central tower, which he rebuilt in brick to replace the crumbling stone.

If you stand by St John of Beverley's grave at the top of the nave and look up, you'll see a large central boss painted in red and gold. Carved not from stone but from wood, it covers a hole in the vault through which building materials were hauled up into the roof space of the tower via a massive wooden treadmill crane. Installed in the 18th century, it was operated by a workman walking, hamster-like, inside the wheel. You can see it if you take the roof tour.

From the mid-19th century massive restoration work took place, much of it under the guidance of Sir George Gilbert Scott, who designed the organ screen (carved by James Elwell of Beverley, who later became the town's mayor). The stained-glass windows are Victorian and memorable, made by the finest stained-glass artists and manufacturers of the era. The windows in all ten bays of the nave aisles pair an event in the life of Christ with one from the Old Testament and repay a close look.

Continuing its long traditions as a place of sanctuary and great music, Beverley Minster lives up to its promise as 'a space for the soul and a feast for eyes and ears'.

BRISTOL CATHEDRAL

Founded as St Augustine's Abbey in 1140, the Cathedral Church of the Holy and Undivided Trinity gained cathedral status in 1542. After the dissolution of the monastery three years earlier, King Henry VIII created the new Diocese of Bristol after, it is said, much lobbying by the citizens of what was by then the most important trading city in England after London. The discovery of a large Anglo-Saxon carved stone during 19th-century rebuilding work, now placed in the south transept, indicates that this had been a Christian site before the Conquest.

There are remains today of the Norman abbey, notably the Abbey Gatehouse on the south side of College Green and the remarkable chapter house, reached from the cathedral cloister, which is a Romanesque gem. With its walls, arches, arcading and vaults so richly carved and intricately patterned in complex geometric designs, it resembles a vast tapestry in stone.

The monastery for Augustinian Canons was founded by a wealthy Bristol merchant and landowner, Robert Fitzharding, the first Lord Berkeley. For the next four centuries the Berkeley family continued their patronage, with most of Fitzharding's successors being buried there. Look for the effigies of Berkeley Lords Thomas and Maurice who were implicated in the rebellion against King Edward II, murdered at their castle.

Built in the early 14th century to replace the Norman abbey, the east end of the cathedral is glorious. The vaulted ceilings of the nave, quire and aisles are all the same height, making it one of the finest examples of a medieval hall church to be seen anywhere. Spacious and light, it was a style favoured in German cathedrals but not often seen in this country. In the quire aisles, the innovative vaulting, its sinuous lines springing from little bridges, is unique to Bristol.

The cathedral has two Lady Chapels. The first, known as the Elder Lady Chapel, was built around 1220 and the carving was the work of masons 'on loan' from Wells Cathedral (page 232). There are interesting little figures in the spandrels, including a fox carrying a goose, sheep musicians and numerous little monkeys.

Originally standing apart from the church, it was incorporated into the north quire aisle during the late 13th- and early 14th-century rebuilding, when the red sandstone Eastern Lady Chapel was designed, at the same time and in the same style as the quire. The chapel was given its Gothic colours by the art historian E.W. Tristram in 1935, in a revival

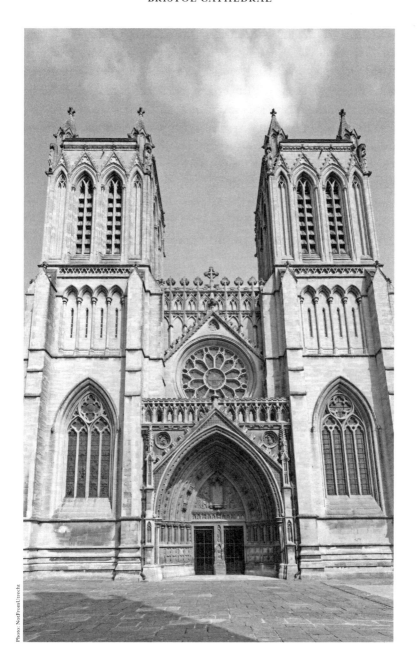

Photo: NotFromUtrecht

of its original splendour. Effigy tombs of 15th-century abbots line the walls.

Framed by the lilting lines of five-pointed stars, stellate tomb recesses are another unique and attractive feature of the cathedral. Their design owes more to the East than the West and as Bristol was an important trading port at the time, and the monks had their own quayside at the harbour, it's likely that ideas for such fine architectural details travelled back with the ships.

Off the south quire aisle, the little sacristy is full of decorative stonework and one of its niches once held an oven for baking communion bread. An unusual doorway leads to the Berkeley Chapel, which has the finest of all the starburst tomb niches. Here you'll find a cathedral treasure, a medieval candelabrum from 1460 crowned by the Virgin Mary and Child. Beneath her St George, clad in the armour of the period, slays the dragon. It came from Bristol's Temple Church, bombed in 1940.

The nave was being rebuilt when the abbey was dissolved by King Henry VIII's commissioners in 1539 and left in ruins, its stone used to build houses right up to the church. It wasn't until the 1860s that a new nave was constructed and the cathedral restored to its original size.

This was the work of the Victorian ecclesiastical architect G. E. Street, in the Gothic Revival style. Partly using the original plans, he wished to marry up the nave with the architecture of the east end, so only the sharp-eyed will discern the Victorian from the medieval. The result is long vistas and a beautiful, light-filled cathedral.

The west front and twin bell towers were added in 1888 by another renowned ecclesiastical architect, John Loughborough Pearson, who designed Truro Cathedral (page 224). He also added the elegant stone-carved quire screen, the fine stone reredos behind the high altar and the pulpit, all perfectly in keeping with the original medieval setting.

New windows were added in the 20th century, some commemorating the roles local people played during the Bristol blitz of 1941. The first 32 women priests in the Church of England were ordained at Bristol Cathedral in March 1994.

BUCKFAST ABBEY

On the edge of Dartmoor, in a gloriously green valley of the River Dart, St Mary's Abbey at Buckfast is a tranquil oasis just off the traffic-roaring Devon Expressway. The only English medieval monastery to be restored and used again for its original purpose, its story is remarkable.

King Cnut founded the original abbey in 1018. Built of wood, it was smaller than most Benedictine monasteries of the time and, judging from the entry in the Domesday Book survey of 1086, a good deal less prosperous.

It was probably in severe decline by 1136 when King Stephen, who sought to revive English monasteries, gave it to the Abbot of Savigny in southern Normandy. Eleven years later, all the Savigniac houses were absorbed into the mighty Cistercian Order. With it came great change.

While life under the Cistercian Rule was austere, the whole monastery and its church were rebuilt in stone on a large scale, with gates to the north and south for travellers to enter through. It grew in importance and wealth, its precincts busy with work and trade. Admitted to the guild

Photo: Sarrapis

of Totnes merchants, the abbey exported large amounts of wool to Italy.

The monks welcomed pilgrims and the merchants who followed the packhorse route through the region. They fished the River Dart, grew rich from the wool trade and farmed the manorial lands. The abbey was also a noted centre of learning and scholarship.

In 1215, King John named the Abbot of Buckfast as custodian of the Crown Jewels. In 1297, Edward I stayed at the abbey, accompanied by a large retinue of soldiers, servants, courtiers and advisors.

More buildings were added. By the 15th century there was a guest hall, a luxurious abbot's lodging where important visitors were entertained and a separate almshouse to care for the needy. The monks ran a school and established fairs and markets to encourage local trade.

After the death of Abbot John Rede in 1535, the last of a long line of abbots all elected by the monks, Gabriel Donne, a close friend of Thomas Cromwell, was imposed on the, by now dwindling, community. He sold off much property, putting in train the process of dissolution.

Two of the king's commissioners and their lawyers arrived in February 1539 to complete the closure. Abbot Gabriel Donne, who signed the deed of surrender, was well rewarded. Over a period of just four months, the commissioners closed 40 West Country monasteries and delivered one and a half tons of gold, gilt and silver to the Tower of London and into the king's coffers.

The abbey's land and estates also fell to the Crown. The manor of Buckfast itself, including its abbey church, was granted to Sir Thomas Denys, a prominent lawyer who amassed great wealth from the estates he acquired after the Dissolution. It remained in his family for 250 years.

Demolition work began immediately and the shell of the monastery was left to crumble. Some of the smaller buildings in the precincts were put to different uses, the almshouse for wool dyeing and the guest hall converted into cottages and a farm. During the 18th century it was a favourite spot for artists who found the ruin romantic.

When mill-owner Samuel Berry bought the site in 1800, he cleared what remained of the rubble in order to build a Gothic-style, castellated mansion, but kept the tower from the abbot's lodgings and 12th-century undercroft. The mansion changed hands four times until, in 1882, its owner decided to sell it, preferably to a religious community.

The advertisement he placed in a Catholic magazine described it as 'a grand acquisition could it be restored to its original purpose.' It was seen by exiled Benedictine monks, who had fled from persecution in France and were living in Ireland.

They lost no time in buying it and set about improving their new monastery's buildings, restoring the abbot's tower and erecting a temporary church (now the chapter house). This was opened in 1884, the year they started work on building a kitchen, refectory and cloister.

In 1903, exactly 365 years after the closure of the original monastery, Boniface Natter was blessed as Abbot. After the ceremony, a cheque for £1,000 was found in the collection basket. This paid for the completion of the west wing, providing much-needed bedrooms.

However, Abbot Natter's greatest wish was to rebuild the Cistercian abbey. One of the monks had discovered part of the medieval foundations while digging in the vegetable garden and subsequently the rest of the foundations were uncovered. An architect drew up plans for the restoration in the style of the mid-12th century, based on studies of other

Cistercian abbeys such as Fountains (page 78), incorporating pointed windows and rounded arches.

Tragically, Abbot Natter drowned in a shipwreck in 1906. His successor, the 30-year-old Anscar Vonier, vowed to bring Natter's wish to fruition. The project leader would be Brother Peter Schrode, who had learned the art of masonry in France, and in January 1907, Abbot Vonier laid the first stone.

For the next 32 years, the builders – usually four monks, never more than six – worked ceaselessly to complete the large church, literally by hand. They began in the traditional way, with the east end, the sanctuary, transepts and two bays of the nave.

Using a horse and cart and stone from a nearby quarry, at first they cut and dressed the stone themselves, using rudimentary tools and mixing mortar in their self-built workshop. Only much later was there enough money to buy the stone ready dressed at the quarry. They made scaffolding by lashing together wooden poles with ropes and chains, lifting the stone manually. The walls were built from platforms 150 feet (45 metres) above the ground, buffeted by the elements and without even the most basic of safety precautions.

The building was financed entirely from donations and funding could be erratic, but work continued throughout the First World War, when the community, two-thirds of whom were German, were prohibited from leaving the monastery except by special licence.

The church was consecrated on 25 August 1932. It was a joyous occasion attended by archbishops, bishops and clergy. The church was packed, so were the precincts, where loudspeakers relayed the service to the crowds outside. The BBC broadcast it to the nation.

However, the building had not been completed. There was still the tower to finish and the fourteen bells, which had been donated in 1910, to install. With the final stone laid on the tower in 1937 it took until December the following year for the pointing to be finished and the last of the scaffolding removed.

Internationally known as a writer, preacher and scholar, Abbot Anscar Vonier had been away on a long lecture tour. He returned, exhausted and ill but happy to see the great work completed. He died three weeks later.

Built from local blue limestone, its window arches, coping stones and turrets in mellow Ham Hill stone, Buckfast Abbey is a beautiful church. In the Norman/Gothic style, with sturdy piers and pointed arches, its interior soars in creamy white Bath stone.

The magnificent nave pavement is an intricate mosaic design of polished marble and granite, designed by Father Charles Norris. A graduate of the Royal College of Art, he painted the stunning lantern tower ceiling in egg tempera and gold leaf in the style of icons and created the spectacular stained glass in the huge east window in the Blessed Sacrament Chapel. Using his innovative method, stained-glass windows have since been made at Buckfast Abbey for churches around the country and abroad.

The high altar and above it the fine Corona Lucis, modelled on medieval versions in German cathedrals, were the work of the German goldsmith, Bernhard Witte in Aachen during the 1920s, as was the bronze baptismal font. Side chapels have intricate designs in gilt and stone; the quire stalls are carved oak in the style of the 15th century. Most of the furnishings for the church were made at the Abbey and donated by individuals.

Outside are large and peaceful gardens, modelled partly on medieval plans. The whole Abbey complex, with its buildings and landscaping, makes a very enjoyable place to visit.

CANTERBURY CATHEDRAL

The Mother Church of the worldwide Anglican Communion, and shrine to the rebirth of Christianity in England, the Cathedral of Christ at Canterbury is host to more than a million visitors a year. Every hour, on the hour, they are asked to be still and join in a prayer – a reminder that, spectacular though the building is, Canterbury Cathedral is very much a working church.

Huge and intricate, overpowering and dramatic, it is a multi-layered cathedral, each level reached by steps shaped by centuries of pilgrim feet. It was the brutal murder, at an altar in his own cathedral, of Archbishop Thomas Becket – by four of King Henry II's knights on 29 December 1170 – and accounts of miraculous healing immediately after his death, that brought the Christian world to its doors in the Middle Ages. Becket's was one of the holiest shrines in all Europe and pilgrimages continue to this day.

Founded in 597, it was rebuilt in 1070 and then largely rebuilt and extended in creamy white Caen stone in 1178. A devastating fire four years earlier had demolished most of the previous cathedral, though the vast and atmospheric 11th-century crypt with its rounded arches and decorated columns, naves, aisles and side chapels, survives to present us with some of the finest Norman stone carvings on pier capitals in England.

They range from geometric to floral to entire stories that are often comical or violent. Look for animal musicians and winged beasts, rams' heads, knights doing battle and a rather appealing lion. The 12th-century wall paintings in the crypt's St Gabriel's Chapel, which include the Archangel Gabriel announcing the birth of John the Baptist to the elderly Zacharias, are the oldest known Christian paintings in the country.

Long, light, tall and graceful, the nave has slim, soaring columns rising to delicate vaulted arches and gilt roof bosses. Looking back you see the glorious west window, its stained glass dating back 800 years; ahead of you, a wide flight of steps leads up to the richly carved, 15th-century stone pulpitum (quire screen) that separates the nave from the quire. Within its niches are original effigies of six English kings that somehow escaped the swords of the Puritans who, during the Civil War of the 1640s, destroyed the accompanying statues of the twelve Apostles during their rampage of destruction through the cathedral. They even stabled their horses in the nave.

Through the screen's archway you get an inspirational view up to the high altar. Stand under the great Bell Harry Tower, and marvel at the stupendous fan vaulting high above you.

From the north-west transept, steps lead down to the Martyrdom Chapel. The site of Becket's murder is marked with a simple altar and a dramatic modern sculpture of jagged swords. Nearby, the circular Corona Chapel, built to house the skull fragment of the crown of the head of St Thomas Becket, sliced off by the sword of one of the attackers, is dedicated to saints and martyrs of our own times.

The powerful quire is Early French Gothic in style, built between 1175 and 1185 and the first major example of Gothic architecture in Britain. The architect, master mason William (Guillaume) de Sens, was badly injured when he fell from scaffolding while inspecting the central roof boss – depicting a lamb and flag in blue and gold, a symbol of the Resurrection – in 1178. His assistant, William the Englishman, continued and completed the work, including the graceful Trinity Chapel behind the high altar.

Photo: Rafa Esteve

The Trinity Chapel is where Becket's relics once rested in a magnificent gold and jewel-encrusted shrine, destroyed in 1538 on the orders of King Henry VIII. Cart loads of treasure boosted the royal coffers – a large ruby, given by the King of France, is now part of the Crown Jewels in the Tower of London.

Two years later, as part of the dissolution of the monasteries, Henry closed down the Benedictine monastery that had surrounded the cathedral since the 10th century. Today a solitary burning candle marks the site of the shrine; the flooring, with its beautiful Italian marble paving, survives and dates from 1220.

The chapel houses the tomb and superb bronze chain-mailed effigy of Edward the Black Prince, eldest son of King Edward III and father of King Richard II, who died in 1376. His military victories, especially over the French in the Battles of Crecy and Poitiers, made him a popular figure at home (though not, unsurprisingly, in France, where he was considered an evil invader and occupier).

Opposite, lies his nephew, King Henry IV (d 1413), the only king to be buried in Canterbury Cathedral, and his wife, Joan of Navarre, Queen of England. Finely detailed alabaster effigies show them side by side, crowned in gold.

Trinity Chapel is also where you'll find St Augustine's Chair, the ceremonial enthronement chair of the Archbishop of Canterbury. Made from one piece of Petworth Marble, it dates from the early 13th century.

Pilgrims to the shrine would have gazed in awe at the luminous stained glass of brilliant hue that portrays miracles attributed to the saint. Roundels in the aptly named Miracle Windows in the ambulatory begin with Becket at prayer and then a storyboard of scenes unfolds to tell of individuals who were cured of maladies from leprosy to blindness and myriad disabilities. Dating from the early 13th century, the colours are extraordinary – intense blues, striking reds, golden yellows, sharp greens – and the figures recognisably lifelike, studied yet full of movement.

Canterbury has a wealth of medieval stained glass. The colours are deep and vibrant and every image tells a story, whether biblical or of the cathedral's own history. Look especially for the Bible and the Miracle Windows, but all of it will stop you in your tracks.

The west window, also known as the Genealogy Window, contains images of early English kings and royal coats of arms, archbishops and, in the tracery lights, an array of Apostles and prophets, all glass from the late 12th or early 13th centuries. The oldest (c1174), Adam Delving in the Garden of Eden, showing Adam as a peasant tilling the soil, is in the bottom row.

In the north quire aisle, two 12th-century Bible windows tell Old and New Testament stories, from Noah releasing the dove to St Peter preaching, the Magi following the star to the parable of the sower, and Christ's miracles, including the Marriage at Cana and the miraculous draught of fish.

When Pope Gregory sent St Augustine and his monks from Rome in 597, to restore the Christian faith to the Saxon English, they landed in Thanet and were welcomed by King Ethelbert (who would soon be baptised by Augustine) and his French Christian wife, Queen Bertha. Augustine was the first Archbishop of Canterbury.

A short walk from the cathedral lie the ruins of St Augustine's Abbey, founded in 598. The abbey, the cathedral and St Martin's church are a World Heritage Site and are linked by Queen Bertha's Walk. St Martin's, believed to date back to Roman times and the oldest church in continuous use in England, is where St Augustine came to worship before he established his monastery.

The cathedral's late medieval cloisters and large chapter house are remnants of the Benedictine monastic buildings. Originally set out by Archbishop Lanfranc in the 11th century and rebuilt in the early 15th, with their heavily ribbed lierne-vaulted ceiling they are fine examples of the Perpendicular style – no surprise perhaps because they were remodelled by Stephen Lote, a pupil of the royal master mason Henry Yevele, who created the stunning nave. Roof bosses and heraldic shields tell of people who contributed to the rebuilding of the cathedral back in the 12th century and modern stained glass, installed in 2014, commemorates modern benefactors to the conservation of the building's fabric.

Lanfranc also built the rectangular chapter house with stone seating for the monks around the walls and a raised chair for the prior. Made from Irish oak, the beautiful early 15th-century wagon-vaulted ceiling was given by Prior Chillenden, as were the stained-glass windows that depict important people in the history of the cathedral.

The top row of the east window shows Queen Bertha, St Augustine and King Ethelbert. King Henry VIII appears second left on the bottom row. The west window depicts scenes from the history of the cathedral, including the murder of Archbishop Thomas Becket, the penance of King Henry II and the move of Becket's bones to his shrine in 1220.

Entry to the cathedral and its precincts is via the impressive, turreted and highly decorated Christ Church Gate, one of the last parts of the monastic buildings to be erected before the Dissolution. Ironically, it may have been built to commemorate the marriage of Prince Arthur, elder brother of King Henry VIII, to Katharine of Aragon in 1502. (The young prince died a few months later and Henry went on to marry Katharine himself.)

Emerge from the gateway and take time to stand and stare. Of the cathedral's three pinnacled towers, the central Bell Harry Tower rises supreme. It dates from between 1493 and 1503, is 235 feet (72 metres) high and is named after the original bell given by Prior Henry. Inside, the exquisite fan vault interior of the tower is one of the most glorious sights of this most memorable of cathedrals.

CHELMSFORD CATHEDRAL

St Mary's Parish Church became the Cathedral Church of St Mary, St Peter and St Cedd in 1914, when a new Church of England diocese for East London was created, with Chelmsford as the seat of its bishop.

From the outside it looks very much the medieval East Anglian parish church, with a square tower, a needle spire and local flint in the walls. That feeling continues as you enter the mid-15th century south porch, its stained-glass windows dedicated to 'tasks and friendships shared', a memorial to the American forces stationed in Essex between 1942 and 1945.

The interior, however, is unexpected. Light and airy, with white walls and elegant arches, there's a sense of openness and space of a kind not usually found in old churches. The 20th-century reordering of the interior – first in 1923 when two eastern bays were added, then in 1983 when its honey-coloured limestone floor was installed, and again in 2000 – has created a welcoming atmosphere. Add in some superb contemporary artwork and you have something rather special.

Photo: Stuart16axe

A striking feature of the nave is the lovely Georgian coved plaster ceiling, patterned and painted in soft shades of blue, pink and gold. It was inserted after the disastrous collapse of the roof and north and south aisles in 1800, when the nave was rebuilt in the original Perpendicular style.

Ahead, a powerful sculpture of Christ in Glory, arms outstretched in welcome, hangs above the chancel arch. Made of oak covered in beaten copper and gilded, it is by Peter Eugene Ball. Seek out further work by this English artist and sculptor in the cathedral: his Mother and Child bas-relief in St Cedd's Chapel at the west end and the cross and candle-stands in the Mildmay Chapel in the east.

In the chancel, the 15th-century roof trusses have been gilded and painted in strong medieval colours, an indication of how brilliantly colourful the old parish church would once have been.

Beneath the east window, which depicts the Virgin Mary and the life and ministry of her Son, there's a splendid patchwork hanging by the influential embroiderer and designer of church textiles, Beryl Dean. Created from 2,220 squares of silk, its colours are taken from those in the window, with five squares of each shade placed together to form a cross. It stands as a backdrop to the Bishop's Chair, crafted from Westmoreland slate by the sculptor John Skelton, who also carved the dean's stall, this time in wood.

The altar is the centrepiece of the chancel, again in Westmoreland green slate. A simple, unembellished design by the architect of the 1983 reordering, Robert Potter (who also made the modern font from the same stone), it weighs one and a half tons.

Flanking it on each side of the chancel arch are two curving bronze and steel ambros (lectern/pulpits) by the renowned sculptor and architectural metalsmith, Giusseppe

Lund. Above them are two icon-style crosses by Sister Petra Clare, a Benedictine nun from Scotland. The Cross of the Seven Doves represents the gifts of the Spirit.

The cathedral houses some truly superb icons. Four in the chancel fill the high blank windows formed when the south transept was added. They portray the saints to whom the cathedral is dedicated, plus Jesus. Those of the Virgin Mary, St Peter and Christ are traditional representations, but that of St Cedd had to be considered afresh.

The missionary St Cedd arrived in East Anglia from Northumbria. He sailed down the east coast from Lindisfarne in 653, landing his boat at Bradwell in Essex. There he founded a Celtic community and in 654 built a small stone church on the foundations of a Roman fort. That same year he was consecrated Bishop of the East Saxons. Isolated on the southern bank of the Blackwater estuary, during the summer months services are still held at St Peter-ad-Muram, St Cedd's tiny cathedral.

In the event St Cedd is portrayed in the tradition of St John the Baptist, holding the Bradwell Chapel in his hands. The iconographers, three Orthodox nuns, completed their work in situ, so the halos look round from ground level and the eyes look down to the viewer.

They also wrote the huge icon of the Ascended Christ in the blue, almond-shaped frame of a mandorla, which hangs above the arch in the north transept. It comes as no surprise to learn that the principal writer of the Chelmsford icons was trained by one of the world's leading authorities on icons.

In the little Mildmay Chapel, to the north of the chancel, a hand-woven tapestry altar frontal traces St Cedd's journey from Lindisfarne to his Bradwell Chapel and finally to Lastingham on the edge of the Yorkshire moors, where he died of the plague. In shades of blue on creamy white, this serene and contemplative scene, reminiscent of the flat Essex coast, took Philip Sanderson of West Dean College in Sussex six months to weave.

Above the altar, the stained-glass windows depict St Cedd and St Alban, the first English martyr. The cathedral banner stands close by. With the finest gold thread stitching and exquisite detail, this embroidery masterpiece by Beryl Dean shows the Virgin Mary in Byzantine style on a background of Indian cloth of gold.

The Mildmay family's prominence in Chelmsford lasted for over 300 years. The brightly coloured Tudor monument to Thomas Mildmay, his wife Avis and their fifteen children stands in the north transept. Having dissolved some of the monasteries in East Anglia for King Henry VIII, Thomas prospered and acquired much land. There's another Mildmay monument around the corner, this time in ornate Rococo marble from the 18th century.

The contemporary artist Mark Cazalet has filled a blank window in the north transept with a giant Tree of Life. Painted on 35 oak panels it is a thought-provoking piece that warrants a close look at the detail. Beneath it in a specially built cabinet is The Living Cross by British iconographer Helen McIldowie-Jenkins, in which the wood of Christ's cross sprouts green leaves.

At the west end of the cathedral, two chapels are separated by the organ loft beneath the tower.

St Peter's Chapel is a memorial to those who suffer in this world. At its heart is 'The Bombed Child', a poignant bronze sculpture by Georg Ehrlich who fled his native Austria for England following the Nazi invasion in 1938. Essex militia and regimental colours hang here and the west window features the patron saints of the armed forces.

The etched window depicting St Peter is by John Hutton,

who engraved the great west screen in Coventry Cathedral (page 59) and the angel doors at Guildford Cathedral (page 97). Giuseppe Lund crafted the bronze screen, also the sculpted bronze railings in St Cedd's Chapel on the other side of the tower.

Here, Mark Cazalet's engraved glass window shows St Cedd, a bearded man with a furrowed brow, amid the building stones of Bradwell. It marked the centenary of the cathedral and diocese in 2014 and the granting of city status to Chelmsford by the Queen two years earlier.

As you leave, take a walk around the church and seek out a very modern stone-carved St Peter, perched on a buttress with his nets and catch, wearing fisherman's boots and holding a Yale key!

Chelmsford Cathedral may not be big (it claims to be the second smallest cathedral in the country) but thanks to the astute and beautiful artwork commissions by a previous dean, it's a gem.

CHICHESTER CATHEDRAL

The joy of Chichester's Cathedral of the Holy Trinity is the way that modern works of art have been incorporated, to great effect, amid Norman arches, Romanesque stone-carved panels and fine medieval effigies.

The vivid colours of John Piper's tapestry on the theme of the Holy Trinity, behind the modern high altar, bring the church to life; Marc Chagall's stained-glass window of praise feels aflame with red, while a huge abstract tapestry, a symbol of Anglo-German reconciliation, forms a powerful backdrop to the altar at the site of St Richard of Chichester's shrine. Graham Sutherland's painting of Christ appearing to Mary Magdalene on Easter morning, *Noli me Tangere*, is a thoughtful contrast to the nearby 2nd-century Roman mosaic.

Look for the simple memorial to composer Gustav Holst (1874–1934), who had a close association with the cathedral, and the charming 14th-century table tomb with the effigies of Richard FitzAlan, Earl of Arundel, and his second wife Eleanor holding hands. It inspired Philip Larkin's poem 'An Arundel Tomb'. Don't miss the expressive, wonderfully detailed stone-carved reliefs of the Raising of Lazarus that probably date from the 12th century or the stunning baptismal font in polished Cornish stone with its bowl of beaten copper, designed by John Skelton in 1983.

Outside, the freestanding medieval bell tower, the only one still remaining at any English cathedral, houses the cathedral shop.

The irascible missionary bishop St Wilfrid, in exile from Northumbria, brought Christianity to Sussex in 681, founding an abbey on the coast near Selsey. The Normans transferred the bishopric, establishing the See of Chichester in 1075, and built a cathedral on the site of a Saxon church, using stone from the Isle of Wight. It was consecrated in 1108 but fires and the effects of foundations set on boggy ground resulted in much rebuilding into the 13th century.

The fine spire was added in the 14th century, strengthened by Sir Christopher Wren in the 17th, but collapsed in 1861. Queen Victoria contributed to the cost of its rebuilding – a slightly taller but otherwise faithful reconstruction by Sir George Gilbert Scott – which was completed in 1866. The only medieval English cathedral visible from the sea, the spire is a landmark for sailors.

The elegant nave, essentially Norman in style, has creamy limestone piers with dark, polished Purbeck Marble shafts that lead the eye to the controversial Arundel screen and through its narrow central arch to glimpse the vivid colours of the highlight tapestry behind the high altar.

Created in the 15th century, a whole bay deep and superbly carved from Caen stone, the screen divided the quire, where the services were held, from the nave used by the laity. It was dismantled in 1860 to remove this separation but in the process cracks in the crossing piers were revealed, leading to the collapse of the tower and spire a year later. The return to its original position in 1961 was no less controversial than its removal by the Gothic Revivalists of the mid-19th century.

Behind it, the quire has original 14th-century misericords under the seats and from here you can get the full impact of John Piper's stunning Holy Trinity tapestry, so rich in colour and symbolism. Woven in Felletin, near Aubusson in France, where Graham Sutherland's *Christ in Majesty* had been made for Coventry Cathedral (page 59), it consists of seven panels, each five metres high and one metre wide, and was installed in 1966.

Both transepts are Norman in origin and the window in the south transept is superb. It tells the story of salvation, from Adam and Eve to the Resurrected Christ, revealing events from the Old Testament (on the right) that foreshadowed those in the New Testament, which are shown on the left. The glass is 19th century, set in 14th-century stonework.

Covering one wall of the south transept, the monumental wood panels, painted in the 1530s by local artist Lambert Barnard, are considered to be the largest surviving Tudor paintings of their kind in the country. Surrounded by portraits of English monarchs from William the Conqueror, two scenes show events in the cathedral's history.

Photo: Tony Hisgett

On the left we see Bishop Wilfrid asking Cædwalla, King of Wessex, for permission to build a church at Selsey. On the right, Bishop Robert Sherborne, who commissioned the paintings, is depicted asking King Henry VIII to guarantee the future of the cathedral after his split with Rome.

Look for the monkey with a wedding ring at its feet in the left scene. This is believed to be a metaphor for Katharine of Aragon, who was known to have a pet monkey, and the discarded ring shows Bishop Sherborne's disapproval of Henry's abandonment of his queen. As the Bishop had travelled to Rome twenty years earlier to persuade the Pope to allow the marriage of Henry and Katharine, the divorce was deeply upsetting to him. Not only that, the impending Reformation threatened his beloved cathedral.

Butler's paintings of the Bishops of Chichester and Selsey line a wall of the north transept. All of the paintings have the same face – that of the artist's patron, Bishop Sherborne.

The shrine of St Richard is given pride of place in the retroquire behind the high altar. The saintly bishop, Richard of Chichester, died in 1253 and his shrine attracted thousands of pilgrims until it was desecrated and destroyed in 1538 during the Reformation, its riches transferred to the Tower of London. Canonised in 1262, he is the patron saint of Sussex.

His shrine area is a model of modern simplicity. On a raised platform, a powerful tapestry designed by Ursula Benker-Schirmer in 1985 forms a backdrop to the Purbeck Marble altar and tall cast-aluminium candlesticks. Woven partly in Germany and partly at nearby West Dean College, it is known as the Anglo-German tapestry and symbolises reconciliation. A 1970s icon of St Richard by Sergei Fyodorov adds further inspiration.

The saint's legacy today comes in the words of his prayer,

perhaps more familiar as 'Day by Day', the popular song from the musical *Godspell*: 'may I know thee more clearly, love thee more dearly, and follow thee more nearly.'

Ahead is the large and peaceful 14th-century Lady Chapel, restored in 2009 to include some of the colour that would have been seen in medieval times. Flanking it, two chapels have modern altar paintings: Graham Sutherland's depiction of the newly resurrected Christ appearing to Mary Magdalene and Patrick Procktor's image of the Baptism of Christ in the Chapel of St John the Baptist.

Then there is Marc Chagall's gloriously uplifting window to ponder. On a vibrant red background, the design is a visual interpretation of Psalm 150: 'Let everything that hath breath praise the Lord'.

Chichester Cathedral is unusual in having two aisles on each side of the nave, a popular feature of churches in France, but not on this side of the Channel. Memorial chapels in the outer aisles pay tribute to members of the Royal Sussex Regiment, the Royal Air Force and the people of Sussex who lost their lives at sea in the Second World War.

This is a popular and much-loved cathedral, happily blending the ancient and the modern, with stories from every century to discover and enjoy.

CHRIST CHURCH CATHEDRAL, OXFORD

Oxford's Cathedral comes as a surprise. Rather than standing boldly at the heart of the city, it is tucked away in the grounds of Christ Church, Oxford University's largest college, alongside its grandest quadrangle, Tom Quad (named after the great bell that hangs in Sir Christopher Wren's crowning clock tower). Also, it is not as big as you might imagine – it is the smallest medieval cathedral in England – which gives it an unexpected intimacy.

In honey-coloured Cotswold limestone, the building dates from the late 12th century. However, its story goes back to the 8th century when St Frideswide, an Anglo-Saxon princess, established a nunnery on the site.

Legend tells that Frideswide hid in the woods to escape the attentions of the powerful and debauched King Algar. When she emerged three years later and found he was still waiting, a thunderbolt blinded him, and he got the message. Several miracles were attributed to her, she was canonised and went on to become the patron saint of both the city of Oxford and the University.

Frideswide's nunnery was destroyed by Danes in 1002 but was later re-established for Augustinian Canons. Their priory church was built around 1180, with the saint's bones translated with much pomp and ceremony to a shrine, where over the years many miracles were noted. Among the pilgrims who visited was Katharine of Aragon, who came to pray for a son, sadly to no avail.

Cardinal Thomas Wolsey (1474–1530) was at the height of his wealth and power when he determined to create a magnificent new college in Oxford, equal in splendour to his palace at Hampton Court and named in his honour. It would have a vast chapel that would outdo King's College Chapel in Cambridge (page 112). The Canons were ejected and three bays of the nave of their church and part of the cloister demolished to make way for Tom Quad and the new college.

By the time of Wolsey's fall from favour in 1529, having been unsuccessful in arranging King Henry VIII's divorce from Katharine of Aragon, only the quadrangle and hall had been built. In 1546 Henry refounded Cardinal College, naming it Christ Church, and declared the truncated church a cathedral. Thus Christ Church is, uniquely, both the college chapel and the Mother Church of the diocese of Oxford.

The massive piers and arcades in the nave, chancel and transept are decisively Norman but unusual in their split capitals, double arches and positioning of the triforium to give an illusion of height. Also unusual, the quire stalls are in the nave, rather than the chancel, and the pews face each other across the aisle, college style. (One further quirk – the cathedral keeps the old 'Oxford time', being five minutes behind GMT, which can be confusing to visitors attending services.)

The colourful Jonah Window to the left as you enter was the work of a 17th-century Dutch artist, Abraham van Linge. Only the figure of Jonah under a gourd tree is made from stained glass. The rest of the window, with the city of Nineveh shown in great detail, was painted.

The cathedral's biggest stained-glass window is in the north transept. It is Victorian and shows the Archangel Michael leading his army of angels to defeat the Devil, illustrating a scene from the apocalyptic New Testament Book of Revelation.

Ahead is the Early Gothic Latin Chapel, so called because services there were defiantly held in Latin right up to 1861. It holds the reconstructed shrine of St Frideswide, covered in stone-carved foliage and faces. The original shrine, which held the relics of the saint, was smashed in 1538 during the Reformation. Over 300 years later, fragments were found lining a well and it was meticulously reassembled.

Alongside it is a splendid 'watching loft' from the 1500s, beautifully carved, half in stone and half in wood, crowned with a forest of pinnacles. A monk would have been in there keeping an eye on pilgrims as they passed, ensuring

Photo: Newton2

no 'souvenirs' were removed. Watching lofts were often features of churches displaying venerated relics, but few have survived. That in St Albans Cathedral (page 161) dates from around 1400.

Above the shrine, the legend of the saintly Frideswide is told in vibrant stained glass by a young Edward Burne-Jones. There are four more windows by this Pre-Raphaelite artist in the cathedral and it is interesting to see the development of his style.

Nearby, a small chapel is dedicated to the memory of Bishop George Bell, a former member of the college. A strong opponent of Nazism, he campaigned against the bombing of German civilians in the Second World War and worked tirelessly for reconciliation. The altar is made from a single piece of 17th-century oak from Windsor Great Park, given by the Queen, with a cross cut from its underside standing nearby.

As you step into the chancel, look up and marvel at the beautiful vaulted ceiling. Its stone ribs splay out from gravity-defying pendants, small intersecting ribs create eight-pointed stars and carved stone bosses reflect personages of the church from Frideswide and the Virgin and Child, through bishops and archbishops and finally, above the Victorian high altar, Jesus. This sensational architectural feat was created in 1500 by Oxford master mason William Orchard.

St Catherine of Alexandria, the patron saint of scholars, is depicted in the Burne-Jones Window of the Chapel of Remembrance. The face of the saint is modelled on Edith Liddell, daughter of the then Dean of Christ Church and the younger sister of Alice Liddell, who was the inspiration for Lewis Carroll's *Alice's Adventures in Wonderland*. The author, whose real name was Charles Lutwidge Dodgson, was a contemporary of Dean Liddell and lectured in mathematics at the college.

The Becket Window in St Lucy's Chapel in the south transept dates from around 1320. It contains a rare panel showing the martyrdom of Archbishop Thomas Becket in Canterbury Cathedral (page 37). King Henry VIII ordered that all images of the 'turbulent priest' should be erased, but this one survived due to quick thinking – the saint's face was replaced with plain glass. To find it, look for the small central blue panel in the upper tracery.

The monuments in the chapel are to men who died fighting for Charles I in the English Civil War of the 1640s. Oxford was the king's headquarters and he lived in the Deanery at Christ Church, attending services and holding some of his parliaments in the Great Hall. During his stay the cathedral silver was melted down to pay for his army.

Steps from the south transept lead down to the cloister and chapter house. Built in 1150, its Romanesque doorway with distinctive carvings is the oldest part of the cathedral and the interior is splendid, but as it now houses the cathedral shop, very few visitors notice!

The best view of the cathedral's spire is from the cloister garden. The oldest surviving stone spire in England, it dates from 1230.

You reach Christ Church Cathedral via college buildings. There's a designated tourist route with admission tickets including entrance to the quads and Wolsey's magnificent Hall – which may look familiar, as a replica of its Renaissance splendour featured as the dining hall in the Harry Potter films.

COVENTRY CATHEDRAL

The German Luftwaffe's prolonged bombing raid on Coventry on the night of 14 November 1940 devastated the historic city. As the incendiary bombs rained down, its cathedral burned with it. The next morning, Richard Howard, the visionary Provost of the time, put his hand in the ashes and wrote the words 'Father forgive' on the blackened wall of the sanctuary. He vowed to rebuild the cathedral as a sign of faith, trust and hope for the future of the world and to work for reconciliation.

Before it was designated Coventry's cathedral in 1918, St Michael's, dating from the 14th century, had been the largest parish church in England, a wonder of Perpendicular Gothic architecture. Its windows were painted by John Thornton who went on to work on the glass in York Minster (page 258).

While most of the building lay in ruins, the splendidly carved 15th-century tower and spire stood their ground, and together with the shell of outer walls and skeletal tracery form a dramatic, thought-provoking ensemble framed against the sky. The 295-foot- (90-metre-) spire is still the tallest structure in the city.

In 1950, over 200 architects submitted drawings in the competition held to design a new cathedral. Basil Spence, later knighted for his work, won with his plan to keep the ruins as a garden of remembrance and to incorporate them into the design of the new building.

His use of the same pink-red Staffordshire sandstone expressed continuity and brought visual unity to the ensemble. Spence's determination to have the new building seemingly arising from the ruins of the old meant that the cathedral must face north/south (instead of the traditional east/west alignment).

Queen Elizabeth II laid the foundation stone in March 1956 and the new cathedral was consecrated in her presence in May 1962. To mark the occasion, Benjamin Britten's specially composed 'War Requiem' received its premiere in the cathedral.

At the entrance, a monumental porch and steps link the old and new structures. A 70-foot- (21-metre-) high clear glass screen, engraved with Old and New Testament figures, saints, martyrs and angels, allows visitors to view the inside of the new cathedral with a reflection of the old.

Guarding the steps, a powerful bronze sculpture, 'St Michael and the Devil', symbolises the strength of good over evil. Depicting the archangel standing triumphant and victorious over a cowering Lucifer, it is by Sir Jacob Epstein, one of several leading British artists and sculptors of the time to contribute fine work to the new cathedral.

Stained-glass windows angled in zigzag walls direct light down the nave towards the altar and the immense tapestry, Christ in Glory. Designed by Graham Sutherland, who in the preceding years had worked as an official war artist recording the effects of German bombing on Britain, it measures 75 feet by 38 feet (23 metres by 11.5 metres), and weighs over a ton. Woven near Aubusson in France and using about 900 colours, it is said to be the largest tapestry in the world to be woven in one piece.

Drawing on the Byzantine Christ Pantocrator, the image is of a very human Christ, Risen in Glory, hands raised in blessing, eyes encompassing all before him. He is flanked by the traditional symbols of the Four Evangelists; the human figure at his feet seems tiny, but in fact is life-sized.

Photo: Steve Cadman

Of brilliant hue and full of symbolism, the ten 70-foot-(21-metre-) high angled side windows only become visible when you walk back down the nave from the altar but John Piper's phenomenal Baptistry Window (to your right as you enter the cathedral) has immediate impact.

An entire wall of stained glass, its vivid colours moving from the outer reds, blues and greens to a sunburst of gold and white at the centre, each of the 195 individual windows contains an abstract design and the overall effect is mesmerising. A large boulder brought from a hillside near Bethlehem forms the font at its feet.

Following the aisle from the Baptistry to the altar brings you to the serenely beautiful Chapel of Christ in Gethsemane. Seen through a crown of thorns made from iron, it shows a kneeling angel in gold mosaic offering the cup of suffering to Christ as he prays.

Provost Richard Howard's vision back in 1940 was for a new cathedral that would be at the heart of a movement for peace and reconciliation between all people of all faiths. Seeing how in wartime Christians of all denominations came together to pray, he conceived the idea of an ecumenical space within the new cathedral – a revolutionary idea at the time. It came to fruition in the Chapel of Unity, a star-shaped building attached to the cathedral. Its colourful mosaic floor, donated by the people of Sweden, represents the nations of the world and is lit by shafts of light from narrow, stained-glass windows.

Coventry Cathedral has indeed become a global symbol of peace and reconciliation, not least in its Community of the Cross of Nails that furthers the work of global peace and dialogue. After the destruction of 1940, Howard fashioned a cross from three nails he found in the medieval roof timbers and since then similar crosses have been given to churches around the world, symbolising new life and friendship out of enmity. One is in the wonderful Kaiser Wilhelm Memorial Church in Berlin, destroyed by Allied bombing, and like Coventry rebuilt as a contemporary church integrating the ruins of the old.

It was a controversial building from the start, and still divides opinion, but a national poll in 1990 showed Coventry Cathedral to be the UK's favourite 20th-century building and it is listed as one of 21 British landmarks for the 21st century.

DURHAM CATHEDRAL

On its peninsula ridge above the wooded cliffs that rise up sheer from the fast-flowing River Wear, the Cathedral of Christ, Blessed Mary the Virgin and St Cuthbert, Durham stands rock solid, a golden sandstone elegy to power and strength. Inside, that show of strength pervades in the unforgettable pillars that line the 11th-century nave. They are almost 22 feet (6.6 metres) round, the same distance high, and deeply carved in bold geometric patterns.

Full of architectural achievements way ahead of its time, the cathedral's early monastic history is revealed not least in the slab of black marble set in the nave's floor that marked the point beyond which no women were allowed to step.

Topped and tailed by two splendid chapels – the Galilee, or Lady Chapel at the west end with its 12th-century wall paintings, medieval glass and tomb of the great historian and scholar the Venerable Bede, and the spacious, stained-glass-filled Chapel of Nine Altars at the east end, overlooked by St Cuthbert's shrine – it is a church of surprises.

There's vibrant, modern stained glass that reflects the local community's involvement in a church for today; its interest in the wider world is revealed by a beautiful banner from Lesotho in Southern Africa, woven to commemorate the cathedral's 900th birthday.

Prior Castell's glorious Tudor clock in the south transept dates from the early 16th century and survived the Civil War. It is huge, ornate, brilliantly colourful and tells the time of day, the day of the month and the phases of the moon. Look carefully at the face – it has 48 (instead of the usual 60) minute markings.

Much of the cathedral's colour comes from nature, from the swirls of cream, gold and orange in the sandstone walls and clear fossil patterns of the local Frosterley stone in the pillars, to the boldly patterned marble floor of the quire.

The magnificent, intricate Neville Screen behind the high altar was carved from Caen stone in the 1370s. Behind that screen is the tomb of the gentle, holy St Cuthbert, the shepherd boy who became Bishop of Lindisfarne and brought the Christian faith to this area of North-east England. He died in 687 and is the reason the cathedral was built.

Cuthbert was revered in Lindisfarne (or Holy Island) but when it came under frequent attacks by Danes, the monks left to seek refuge in Northumbria, carrying with them the body of their Bishop. In 995, so the legend goes, the cart bearing the coffin suddenly stopped and could not be moved. Following a route taken by dairymaids searching for a lost dun (brown) cow, they were led to a rocky outcrop above the River Wear, and once more the cart moved easily. Believing this to be a sign from Cuthbert that this should be his last resting place, the monks built a small church and shrine there. To this day, the road leading up to the hilltop site of Durham Cathedral is called Dun Cow Lane.

After the Norman Conquest in 1066, King William I chose Durham as his preferred location from which to administer the north of his kingdom and protect it against invasion by raiding Scots. Seeing the defensive value of the position of the church holding the relics of the saint, which had by then become a popular pilgrimage site, he ordered the building of a castle, a monastery and a cathedral for the shrine of St Cuthbert.

Work began on the cathedral in 1093 under the command of William of St Calais, whom William the Conqueror had appointed to be the first prince-bishop. For the next almost 800 years, Durham's prince-bishops carried out a secular, as well as religious role, governing and protecting England's northern frontier, often more warriors than churchmen, living like kings and wielding significant power.

William's cathedral was constructed in a mere 40 years, although he did not live to see it, his work being completed by his ambitious successor, Bishop Ranulf Flambard. Although building continued into the 13th century, with the central tower rebuilt in the 15th, the interior of the cathedral we see today remains essentially Norman, a masterpiece of Romanesque architecture.

It's the nave with its avenue of powerful columns, dogtooth arches and decorative zigzagging that remains long in the memory of visitors, but look upwards and you will see one of the most daring innovations of the time.

English cathedrals of this period were built with wooden roofs but Durham's vault is stone, with ribs forming pointed arches to support it, giving the effect of soaring lightness. It was an engineering achievement that marked a turning point in church architecture.

The cathedral suffered during the Reformation as zealots defaced statues and destroyed altars and stained glass.

Photo: Tilman2007

The riches of St Cuthbert's shrine were a prime target. In 1539 the commissioners who came to strip it of its treasure were amazed to discover that, just as the monks had always insisted, St Cuthbert's body was still intact in his tomb.

Today the shrine's simple grey stone, inscribed 'Cuthbertus', has an overhead canopy of vivid 20th-century colours and design. Depicting Christ as a young man, it is by the Scottish-born architect, Sir John Ninian Comper.

During the Civil War some 3,000 Scottish prisoners, captured by Oliver Cromwell, were held in the cathedral following the Battle of Dunbar in 1650. The conditions were appalling and all the woodwork in the great building was damaged or disappeared at this time. It's likely it was burned as firewood by the prisoners, at least half of whom died during their captivity. A mass grave was discovered during construction work on Palace Green, near the cathedral, in 2013.

After the Restoration of the English monarchy in 1660, it was Bishop John Cosin who replaced the quire stalls and towering cover of the marble baptismal font in a style that's a flamboyant mix of Gothic and Jacobean carving.

The Right to Sanctuary was abolished around this time. Under it, a person who had committed a great offence could rap the sanctuary knocker on the cathedral's northern door and be given refuge for 37 days, during which time they would try to reconcile with their enemies or arrange their exile on board a ship from the nearest port.

The original 12th-century sanctuary knocker with its lion-like face and bulging eyes is housed among the cathedral treasures; the one you see at the door now is a bronze replica.

The Benedictine monastery and its priory were closed down in 1539 during Henry VIII's dissolution of the monasteries, but the cathedral retains its cloisters (rebuilt in the 19th century) and boasts some of the most intact surviving 14th-century monastic buildings in England. These are now used to host Open Treasure, a £10 million visitor experience. The long, oak-beamed monks' dormitory is an exhibition space and library while the octagonal-shaped priory kitchen with its high rib-vaulted ceiling has been designed to provide a fitting home for the Treasures of St Cuthbert.

Across the green stands William the Conqueror's great motte-and-bailey castle, founded in 1072, the principal seat of Durham's prince-bishops for almost 800 years and now used by Durham University. Together with Britain's finest Norman cathedral, it is a UNESCO World Heritage Site.

ELY CATHEDRAL

Seen from a far distance across the flat Cambridgeshire fenland, Ely's Cathedral Church of the Holy and Undivided Trinity seems almost ephemeral. Up close it is triumphant. The beautiful simplicity of the nave, the dizzying fan vaulting of the Octagon and Lantern Tower (one of the world's great architectural marvels), the sumptuous painted ceiling, glorious woodcarving and exquisite stone tracing make it a joy to visit.

Ely was an isolated island surrounded by marshland when St Etheldreda founded Ely Abbey in 672. A daughter of King Anna of East Anglia and one of England's earliest female saints, despite two arranged marriages she kept her vow of perpetual virginity and founded a dual monastery for monks and nuns at Ely, ruling as the abbess. She died in 679 and when her coffin was opened years later, her body was found to be uncorrupted and even the cloths she was wrapped in appeared fresh. Her tomb became a popular medieval pilgrimage site, miracles were ascribed to her and the dates of her birth and death are celebrated in the cathedral to this day.

Etheldreda's abbey was sacked by the Danes then refounded as a Benedictine monastery for men in 970. It became one of the richest monasteries in England but was demolished in 1081 by the elderly Abbot Simeon, a relative of William the Conqueror, in order to build an impressive church in the Norman style. It would be a brilliant beacon of faith amid the lawless fens. Before it was even completed it had been designated a cathedral, with the first Bishop of Ely appointed in 1109.

Built from stone brought from Peterborough Abbey's own quarry at Barnack, and Purbeck Marble from Dorset for decorative detail, it is renowned as an outstanding example of English Gothic architecture. A tall (215 feet, 66 metres) castellated and imposing tower with top-to-toe blind arcading dominates the west front; the two turrets of the south-west transept would not look amiss on a fairy tale castle.

Entrance to the cathedral is through the elegant Great West Door in the Galilee Porch. A pavement labyrinth lies boldly beneath the tower. Added in the 19th century, the only one to be found in an English cathedral, it is twenty feet (6.1 metres) across and, unlike a maze, there are no confusing dead ends. To your left, look for 'The Way of Life', a contemporary sculpture in cast aluminium commissioned for the millennium. To your right, the south-west transept is a feast of Romanesque decoration.

Ahead is the long (248-foot, 75-metre) and stunning nave. With twelve bays, alternating in design, and three arcades of rounded arches supported by powerful piers, its cluster pillars rise right up to the clerestory and thus emphasise its height (105 feet, 32 metres). It dates from the early 12th century. The colourful, elaborately painted ceiling, however, is from the major restoration that took place in the mid-19th century. Based on the ancestry of Jesus, it begins with the creation of Adam and ends with the ascended Christ in Majesty, with Old and New Testament narratives, prophets and Evangelists to seek out along the way.

There's a wonderful space at the top of the nave and its style is unique to Ely. In 1322, the Norman central tower collapsed, taking with it the crossing and three bays of the quire. It was a disaster that led to the cathedral's most famous and celebrated feature, the Octagon.

Through the imagination of the monk/architect Alan of Walsingham, working with the royal master carpenter William Hurley, the replacement of the old square tower with a stone octagon crowned by a lantern in wood, lead and glass to suffuse it with light, was not only revolutionary, it was a masterpiece of medieval engineering. It took eighteen years to build and the method of its construction still enthrals architects and engineers. To take a tower tour and get the view down onto the cathedral below is a memorable experience.

On either side of the Octagon, the north and south transepts are the oldest part of the building and contain fine stonework. Look up – the hammer-beam roofs, installed in the 15th century, are decorated with colourful flying angels.

The south transept chapel is dedicated to the two 10th-century bishops who founded the men's monastery in 970, St Dunstan and St Ethelwold. The Benedictine community remained until 1539 when it was disbanded during King Henry VIII's dissolution of the monasteries.

Photo: Hadrianus1959

The rebuilding required by the tower's collapse offered the opportunity to rethink the first three bays of the quire, resulting in a style closer to that of the new Octagon. The rest of the quire stalls are 14th century and have carved wood misericords beneath the seats. These display whole tableaux, from Adam and Eve to the beheading of John the Baptist, as well as single figures of saints and musicians, animals and birds. The desks and front stalls have some fine Victorian-era carvings.

King Henry III and Prince Edward were in attendance when the presbytery behind the quire was dedicated in 1252. The Victorian architect, George Gilbert Scott, designed the Italianate reredos of the high altar during his major restoration of the cathedral, which by the 19th century had fallen badly into disrepair. The delicate quire screen is his, too, and became a model for his work in churches and cathedrals around the country.

The far eastern end of the cathedral is dedicated to St Etheldreda. Elaborate, highly ornate chantry chapels grace the quire aisles, and a millennium project, Processional Way, in the north quire aisle restored the pilgrims' direct link to the Lady Chapel.

Added in the early 14th century and the largest attached to any British cathedral, the Lady Chapel was originally sumptuously decorated with statues, murals and stained-glass windows. Today it is a sad reminder of the desecration wrought during the Reformation in the 16th century, but its vast size, lightness and airiness still have great impact. Arched alcoves line the walls, with exquisite filigree carvings, elaborate tracery and sinuous lierne vaulting on high. The modern statue of Mary above the altar has few admirers.

EXETER CATHEDRAL

A row of angels seems to be supporting two tiers of kings, knights, bishops, Apostles and prophets in the niches above them. Imbued with individual character and energy these sit, stand, turn and pray. Two with their legs crossed appear to be having an argument. All around them are decorative plants and animals. This image screen on the west front of the Cathedral Church of St Peter in Exeter, carved in stone in the 14th century, just hints at the glories to be experienced within.

Stand in the nave and you'll understand why even the pickiest of historians and architects heap praise on Exeter Cathedral. Light floods through windows on to a forest of honey-coloured stone in this most graceful of cathedral interiors.

From west to east it's a vista of lively Decorated Gothic piers, moulded arches and clusters of blue Purbeck Marble shafts, then above in the triforium, an arcade of coloured trefoil arches. Ribs spring from a single capital in each bay, fanning out like palm branches to meet in a central ridge of painted and gilded bosses. At around 315 feet (96 metres), it's the longest uninterrupted medieval vaulted ceiling in the world.

As you approach the altar, cast your eyes upwards to the minstrels' gallery above the nave's north arcade. Built in 1350 it has twelve brightly coloured stone angels enthusiastically playing musical instruments, including a viol, trumpet, tambourine, bagpipes and a recorder.

Most cathedrals have moved the organ to one side, but not Exeter. Supported by the great screen at the top of the nave, it dominates the quire, where the misericords, carved beneath the canons' stalls in the 1250s, are said to be the oldest complete set in England.

The screen, or pulpitum, dates from 1325. In pale Purbeck limestone, its three arches are topped by an openwork arcade filled with a dozen 17th-century painted panels depicting scenes from the life of Christ. Human and animal faces peer out from a riot of foliage in the intricately stone-carved decoration.

A colourful astronomical clock from the late 15th century graces the north transept. The earth is shown in the centre of the dial and the moon revolves around it, turning on its axis to show its phases. A fleur-de-lis depicts the sun and revolves around the earth, pointing to the hour on the outer circle. The small upper dial with a single hand shows the minutes and was added in 1760. A small bell chimes the quarter hours. From high in the tower above, the huge Peter Bell strikes the hour. Look for the round hole in the door below – it's a medieval cat flap.

Also in the north transept is one of Exeter's three early 16th-century chantry chapels. This is the Sylke Chantry from 1508 and has Tudor carving and wall painting. The highly ornate Speke Chantry (known as the Chapel of St George) is in the north quire aisle. Opposite, in the south quire aisle, the Chapel of St Saviour commemorates Bishop Oldham, founder of Manchester Grammar School. Look for the tiny owls amid the carving.

The bishop's throne (*cathedra*) in the quire, carved from Devon oak in the early 14th century and towering to a pinnacled height of 60 feet (eighteen metres), is a masterpiece of the skilled woodcarver's art.

When Prince William of Orange invaded England in 1688, having landed in Brixham and travelled to Exeter, it was from this throne that his 'declaration of peaceful intent' was read. Shortly afterwards he and his wife were declared joint rulers as King William III and Queen Mary II.

The quire stalls are a good Victorian reconstruction but the carved canopies, ornate sedilia (clergy seats) and the misericords – a collection of fantastical creatures, sirens, centaurs, dragons, even an elephant (with horses hooves) – are original, from the late 13th and early 14th centuries.

Behind the high altar, two arches give a glimpse into the retroquire and form the base of the great east window. Much of the glass is medieval, with nine of the figures dating from 1304. At the cathedral's east end, the glorious Lady Chapel has modern glass depicting the life of the Virgin Mary.

The diocese of Devon and Cornwall, with Exeter as its bishop's seat (cathedral), was established in 1050. There had been a Saxon minster on the site, which the Danes destroyed in 1003 and King Cnut rebuilt in 1019.

When William the Conqueror's nephew, William Warelwast, became Bishop of Exeter in 1107, he built a large Romanesque cathedral. Its turreted twin towers were incorporated into the cathedral that replaced it, the one we see today. About halfway down the building they flank its north and south sides and their interiors form the transepts – a unique arrangement in English cathedrals and a defining and much celebrated feature at Exeter.

By the time construction of the current cathedral started in 1275, the latest style in architecture was English Decorated Gothic, hence the rich carvings and large windows, their tracery some of the most innovative in existence.

In 1316, Thomas of Witney, master mason at Winchester (page 245) and renowned as the finest English architect of the day, took charge. His greatest legacies to be seen today are the extraordinary bishop's throne, which took three years

to complete, the lavish and gilded sedilia and the intricately carved stone pulpitum.

The image screen on the west front, installed by Bishop John Grandison as his personal stamp on the cathedral's architecture, was to be the final addition. Some of the statues were in place by 1348 when the Black Death claimed the lives of its designer, William Joy, and his masons. Work restarted in the 1370s but it was only completed around a century later.

Exeter Cathedral has a grand collection of elaborate tombs with brightly coloured effigies and many memorials. The most recent of these, unveiled in 2017, is the memorial to the Polish airmen of 307 Squadron. Heavily outnumbered night fighters, they defended the city during the revenge bombing blitz on Exeter by the Luftwaffe in 1942.

One bomb reduced the Chapel of St James to rubble; 2,000 tons of masonry came crashing down and made the quire unstable. On a post-war visit to see work on its reconstruction, King George VI called it 'the greatest jigsaw puzzle in the world'.

Its design follows that of the medieval original, with a few 20th-century additions in the carvings. The master mason at the time, George Down, is depicted with his stonemason's tools and the carved head of a rugby player commemorates a match in 1951 between Exeter Rugby Club and Oxford University to raise funds for the cathedral's restoration.

The original charter for the foundation of the cathedral in 1050 is preserved in the library archives, as is the Exon Domesday, containing information about politics, society and the landscape of south-west England a thousand years ago. But perhaps its greatest treasure is the Exeter Book, a 10th-century anthology of poetry in Old English that's probably the oldest book of English literature in the world.

The library and archives are housed in the west wing of the Bishop's Palace, with thousands of books and manuscripts spanning eleven centuries.

It's the balance and symmetry of the architecture that makes Exeter Cathedral so special: each window and chapel on one side has its counterpart on the other. The Norman tower transepts, too, mirror each other, while the whole nave seems to flow seamlessly into the distance. Add to this its setting, a wide grassy green close untroubled by traffic, and should there be such a thing as the perfect English cathedral, Exeter might just fit the bill.

FOUNTAINS ABBEY

The largest and probably the best-known monastic ruins in England, Fountains Abbey presents a dramatic, wonderfully atmospheric sight. The setting, on the floor of a wooded valley with the River Skell flowing through it, is beautiful.

Medieval monasteries in England followed the Benedictine Rule, written by St Benedict in the 6th century and reformed in the 10th century. By the 12th century, however, many abbeys had moved away from the discipline and simplicity of the rule and embraced a wealthy lifestyle.

A new order, the Cistercians, formed in Burgundy and committed to returning to the austerity demanded by St Benedict, reached England in 1128. Their emphasis was on prayer, manual labour and self-sufficiency.

In the winter of 1132, led by Prior Richard, thirteen monks from the Benedictine Abbey of St Mary in York fled to the Archbishop's Palace in Ripon, seeking a place where they could live a devout and contemplative life. They were given land on a wild site 'thick set with thorns' in the remote Skell Valley on which to start a new abbey.

Survival there was difficult and they sent to France, to Bernard, the Abbot of Clairvaux, asking to join the Cistercian family. With the first Cistercian abbey in Yorkshire established at Rievaulx a few years earlier, Bernard offered support and sent a skilled builder (architect) to help. In the meantime, the Dean and two Canons of York, all wealthy men, arrived to join the little community at Fountains.

Now they had the funds and the knowledge, building of the abbey began in 1134, using timber from the surrounding trees and sandstone from the steep valley sides. A fire in 1147 destroyed the wooden buildings and damaged the church, which was immediately rebuilt. The great Abbey Church with its imposing west front and the cloister with its beautiful rounded arches were completed around 1160.

The Cistercians built all their abbeys according to a similar plan – stark, functional and undecorated – which reflected their strict and austere way of life. They were also unusual in having lay brothers, who worked in agriculture, building and the trades and crafts essential to the day-to-day running of a monastery, while the monks devoted their days to prayer. Beginning with a vigil at 2am they attended seven services a day, from daybreak to dusk.

The monks wore simple white habits made from rough, undyed sheep's wool. Underwear was forbidden, food rations were sparse and with long periods of enforced silence, communication was mainly by sign language.

The lay brothers wore dark brown tunics for their manual work. Although they had taken monastic vows, they had their own dormitory, refectory and infirmary and attended fewer services, which were held in the nave of the church. Up to

200 lay brothers would have slept in the dormitory and many more lived on farms on the estates the abbey accumulated.

It was mainly thanks to them that during the 13th century, Fountains Abbey became one of the richest and most influential religious houses in England, its wealth coming mainly from the sale of wool to Flanders and Italy. Income also came from cattle rearing and horse breeding, quarrying and mining.

As the abbey's wealth and power grew, so did the building work. Wealthy patrons who donated sizeable parcels of land were accommodated in two-storey guesthouses in the abbey grounds. Ordinary visitors would have stayed in the large aisled hall.

The eastern arm of the church was rebuilt in the mid-1200s, becoming more ornate with nine altars or small chapels. The great window and carvings were the result of a programme of rebuilding under Abbot Darnton in the late 1400s.

Unusually for a Cistercian abbey, a 167-foot- (51-metre-) tall bell tower, its windows decorated with stone carvings and statues, was added to the north transept around 1500. Known as Huby's Tower, it was built in local limestone by the reforming Abbot Marmaduke Huby and is a dominating feature of the ruins today.

The Abbey was at its peak in the 13th century but then disaster followed. Mismanagement of funds led to debts, there were raids by Scots ravaged by famine, harvests failed and the sheep that provided so much of the wealth succumbed to disease. Then the Black Death in 1349–50 carried off many of the monks and a large number of lay brothers. With not enough labour to work the farms, much of the land was rented out.

Finally the arrival of powerful abbots in the late 1400s reversed its fortunes. Abbot Huby in particular introduced

Photo: mattbuck

reforms that set it back on track and gave Fountains its final prosperity in the early Tudor period.

But the days of the monasteries were numbered as King Henry VIII seized their assets and closed them down. At Fountains Abbey the deed of surrender was signed in the chapter house in November 1539. Sold to a wealthy London merchant, everything that could be taken was removed, from the lead to the glass in the windows, and the roofs of the buildings torn down. Land was leased out to tenants; outbuildings fell into disrepair. Stone was there for the taking.

So it remained until the 1760s when William Aislabie, MP for Ripon, took ownership. Combining his own estate at Studley Royal with that of Fountains, he incorporated the abbey ruins into the spectacular gardens he and his father were creating.

One building escaped the closure of the abbey and that was Fountains Mill. Built in the 12th century to grind grain for the monastery, it was in use right up to 1927. Restored, it houses an interactive exhibition.

The ruins today are a vision of towering walls and soaring Early English Gothic arches; of solidly crafted, round-arched doorways and long arcades. Beneath the lay brothers' range, a spectacular vaulted cellarium stretches to over 300 feet (91 metres).

An award-winning interpretation centre in the Porter's Lodge, inside the original gatehouse, tells the story of Fountains and contains a model of how the Abbey would have looked before the dissolution of the monasteries.

In the care of the National Trust, Fountains Abbey and Studley Royal Water Garden is a UNESCO World Heritage Site.

In the spectacular 18th-century pleasure gardens, the winding waters of the River Skell are channelled past the abbey ruins into serene ponds and mirrored lakes, framed by trees. Paths meander by the lake and cascade, past temples, follies, statues and the Palladian Banqueting House, often revealing surprise vistas.

Also on this vast estate: Fountains Hall, an Elizabethan mansion partly built from stone from the abbey ruins and, at the highest point of the Deer Park, the magnificent Victorian church of St Mary, decorated in the richly coloured Gothic Revival style of the 1870s.

GLASTONBURY ABBEY

Steeped in myth and legend, Glastonbury is probably England's most famous abbey. It was the richest at the time of the Domesday Book in 1086 and second only to Westminster Abbey by the time it was dissolved by King Henry VIII in 1539. Abbot Whyting was one of the few in England who resisted the king's command and he and two monks came to a very nasty end at the top of nearby Glastonbury Tor.

Today the ruins give some indication of its size and grandeur. Archaeological excavations have resulted in many fascinating discoveries, revealed in the well-designed and informative museum that you pass through before stepping out into the 36 acres of parkland with its trees, orchards, herb garden and fishponds.

Mostly recovered during excavations since 1908, the museum's collections include worked stone and painted plaster, ceramic tiles, window glass and pottery. They are displayed to illustrate the story of the Abbey, the lives of its monks and pilgrims and of course its legends.

Piecing together its history isn't easy. Tradition has it that Joseph of Arimathea, who provided the tomb in which Christ was buried, arrived in Glastonbury with two vials containing drops of Christ's blood and the chalice used at the Last Supper (the Holy Grail), and founded a small wattle and daub church there in AD 63. An alternative story is that it was Christian missionaries from Rome who built a church in the 2nd century.

That there were early settlements here is not in doubt. Glastonbury Tor had been a sacred site before the arrival of Christianity. Before the Somerset Levels were drained, this was a watery region of islands and marsh, which attracted hermits. A sacred well, fed by a spring that never ran dry, was named the Chalice Well in Christian times.

Finds within the site have included Iron Age pottery and Roman objects, there's archaeological evidence for timber structures dating to around AD 500, while excavations in the 1920s revealed three phases of stone churches associated with a Saxon monastery, the earliest dated to around 700.

History becomes a little clearer in the 10th century, when the abbey's most famous abbot, St Dunstan (909–88), created a Benedictine monastery modelled on that at Cluny in Burgundy, making it a noted centre of learning and manuscript production. That it gained royal favour is witnessed by the burial there of three kings of Wessex between 946 and 1016. A noted reformer, Dunstan went on to be Bishop of Worcester, Bishop of London and in 960, Archbishop of Canterbury.

After the Conquest, the Normans went on a massive building spree throughout the land. The first Norman abbot's changes in liturgy and lifestyle, and the substantial additions to Glastonbury Abbey, did not go down well with the monks, who staged a protest and bloody battle in the church.

It was under the fourth abbot, the powerful Henry of Blois, grandson of William the Conqueror, nephew of King Henry I and younger brother of King Stephen, that the abbey reached its greatest prestige.

During his long tenure he was made Bishop of Winchester and with his passion for architecture built castles and extensions to palaces. He loved literature, too, commissioning the history of the abbey from the chronicler William of Malmesbury and sponsoring the Winchester Bible (page 245). After his death, disaster struck. In 1184 a raging fire destroyed his beloved abbey.

The Lady Chapel was built immediately after the fire, ready for use in 1186. It stands on the site of the wooden 'old church', placing it to the west end of the Great Church rather than the traditional east end. The most sacred part of the medieval abbey, and the most complete of its ruins, it is considered one of the finest late 12th-century monuments in England.

Its walls survive to full height and some of the delicate sculpted stone can still be seen. The Romanesque rounded arch above the north door is superb, with five orders of decorative carving depicting scenes from the life of the Virgin Mary between bands of richly-detailed foliage.

The ruins of the once magnificent Great Church, built in the Early Gothic style, are more fragmentary but do give an indication of its vastness. With a total internal length of 580 feet (176 metres), only Old St Paul's in London was longer.

The intact Abbot's Kitchen is the finest of the monastic buildings and gives an indication of the wealth and prestige of the abbey in the mid-1300s. A square stone structure, it has an eight-sided stone roof rising to an ingenious octagonal lantern, allowing smoke from the four fireplaces below to escape from a central vent.

Now freestanding, it would originally have been part of

Photo: Nilfanion

an extensive Abbot's Complex, with a great hall and palatial palace providing grand accommodation for the powerful abbot and his guests.

The Abbey had always made much of its founding by Joseph of Arimathea and links with tales of King Arthur and his knights in their quest for the Holy Grail, and never more so than in the 12th century.

The contemporary historian Gerald of Wales recorded that in 1191 the monks had discovered the grave of King Arthur and Queen Guinevere. Given the timing, so soon after the disastrous fire, when money was needed to rebuild their church, modern historians consider that the exhumation was probably faked.

It wasn't until 1278, when the nave of the Great Church had been completed, that the bones were reburied in a marble tomb and placed in the quire before the high altar, in a ceremony attended by King Edward I and Queen Eleanor. It survived until the dissolution of the abbey.

The abbey may have crumbled but the legends continued to evolve and flourish. The story of the Glastonbury Thorn was strong in the 17th century. It tells that when Joseph of Arimathea arrived in Glastonbury he rested on Wearyall Hill, thrusting his staff into the ground, where it sprouted into a thorn tree.

The tree, and others grafted from it, blossom twice a year, in spring (Easter) and winter (Christmas), thus it was considered a Holy Thorn. The tradition of presenting a sprig to the reigning monarch on Christmas Day was revived in the 1920s and continues to this day.

William Blake's poem 'And did those feet in ancient time', set to music by Sir Hubert Parry as 'Jerusalem', revived the legend that the boy Jesus travelled with Joseph of Arimathea on one of his earlier visits to the area.

After the execution of Abbot Whyting, the riches of Glastonbury Abbey were quickly carted off to further enrich the King, and stone from its walls was plundered by the townspeople. The site passed through several owners until 1906, when it returned to the Church, bought on behalf of the Bishop of Bath and Wells.

GLOUCESTER CATHEDRAL

Boasting the finest cloisters in England with the first fan vaulting ever built, one of the largest and most spectacular of medieval stained-glass windows anywhere in the country, and the pinnacled tomb of a murdered king, Gloucester's Cathedral Church of St Peter and the Holy and Indivisible Trinity is a story book on history and architecture.

It saw the coronation of the boy-king Henry III in 1216, when he was just nine years old – the only English king since the Norman Conquest not to be crowned in Westminster Abbey – a scene beautifully depicted in a Victorian stained-glass window. William the Conqueror spent the Christmas of 1085 at Gloucester and it was in the chapter house that he formulated the idea of the Domesday Book.

The Abbey of St Peter at Gloucester was founded in 679 by Osric, ruler of the Hwicce tribe. When Serlo, the first Norman abbot, arrived from the Benedictine abbey of Mont St Michel in Normandy in 1072, he found a very depleted monastery – just two monks and six novices.

His first job was to enlarge the community and extend and recover income from the abbey's lands, which he did with some speed. By 1089 he'd begun the building of a new abbey in the Romanesque style. The massive cylindrical columns, 32 feet (ten metres) high and six feet (two metres) in diameter that line the cathedral's nave to the crossing are witness to his work.

The rather splendid organ case above the screen blocks the view to the quire and beyond. Strangely this does the visitor a favour, as the surprise is even greater as you leave the brooding nave and unexpectedly find yourself in a space of soaring lightness.

It was the murder of the deposed king, Edward II, at Berkeley Castle in 1327 that was to trigger the rebuilding of the east end of the abbey church. When his son, King Edward III, seized power from his mother Queen Isabella and her lover Roger Mortimer, he determined that his father should have a fitting memorial. With its canopy of towering, intricately fashioned pinnacles and the king's effigy exquisitely carved in alabaster, it is surely one of the most beautiful royal tombs anywhere.

The King may have been unpopular in life but in death he attracted a vast number of pilgrims and their offerings funded a massive building project in the radical new Perpendicular style of architecture, undertaken by skilled royal masons.

Slender columns soar to a magnificent lierne vault 88 feet (27 metres) above the floor. In the sumptuous quire, bosses on the vault above the high altar show Christ surrounded by an angel choir playing musical instruments.

Then there's the great east window, a wall of medieval glass the size of a tennis court, in colours of cool blue and silver with judicious use of red, so very different from the rich colours usually associated with the Middle Ages.

With a centrepiece of Christ and the Virgin Mary in Glory flanked by the twelve Apostles, and rising to Christ in Majesty at the top, its nine tiers show a medieval hierarchy of saints and martyrs, abbots and bishops, and in the bottom row, the shields of royalty and nobles. When it was installed around 1350 it was the largest window in Europe.

The 15th-century Lady Chapel with its high vaulted roof on a series of stone arches, lit by large stained-glass windows, feels like a church within a church. The series of early 20th-century windows by the Arts and Crafts artist Christopher Whall are considered to be the finest glass of the period in England.

Its two chantry chapels have much more recent windows: one in memory of Gloucester musicians and the composer Herbert Howells, the other a Tom Denny installation from 2014 commemorating the local First World War poet and composer Ivor Gurney. The Norman lead font, dating from around 1140, is still in use today.

In the south transept, look for the medieval bracket thought to be a memorial to an apprentice who fell from the vault above. L-shaped, like a mason's set square, it shows the master mason looking up in horror. Then do step into the brilliantly colourful St Andrew's Chapel. It was decorated in high Victorian neo-Gothic style by Thomas Gambier Parry, who painted the lantern of Ely Cathedral (page 68).

The tomb-like memorial to King Osric, depicted holding a model of his abbey church, stands close to King Edward II's magnificent tomb while on the other side of the quire there's the colourful effigy of Robert, Duke of Normandy, eldest son of William the Conqueror. In life he was in constant conflict with King Henry I, his youngest brother, and here he is depicted about to draw his sword.

The abbey's royal connections probably saved it from destruction. During the Reformation, King Henry VIII established a new Diocese of Gloucester and designated the building Gloucester Cathedral.

Photo: Mango salsa

Today, the cathedral is probably best known for its spectacular, fan-vaulted cloisters. Created in the new Perpendicular style by Thomas of Cambridge in the 1350s, almost 200 years before King's College Chapel's glorious fan vault would come to fruition (page 112), the dazzlingly intricate stone work in all four of its walks seems to defy adequate description.

You can still see the long stone basin that was the monks' communal washing place (*lavatorium*), complete with recesses for their towels, and a row of twenty carrels where the monks would sit and study, with windows looking out onto the garden. Step into this calm oasis and enjoy its peace – and view of the very fine 15th-century tower.

GREAT ST MARY'S, CAMBRIDGE

Known as The University Church Cambridge, town and gown have been meeting at Great St Mary's for over 800 years. A parish church just off the market square in the very heart of the city – in the first written record of 1205 it was named 'St Mary's-by-the-market' – it has always been a place of learning, teaching, debate and dispute. With its iron railings smothered in a colourful array of posters and flyers for concerts, talks and events, if you want to know what's going on in Cambridge, this is the place to browse.

When scholars began arriving in the city from Oxford in 1209 they used the nave of the building for lectures, debates and the conferring of degrees. The church has been an important part of the academic and ceremonial life of the University of Cambridge ever since.

Affectionately referred to around town as GSM, Great St Mary's dates from a major rebuilding project in the Perpendicular Gothic style begun in 1468, with the tower being completed much later in 1608. Bishops, abbots and academics contributed to the cost, as did two royal rivals, the Yorkist King Richard III and the Lancastrian King Henry VII.

Henry gave 100 oak trees for the nave roof. Unfortunately they weren't his to give, and the King had to write a letter of abject apology to the Abbot of Westminster who actually owned the forest.

Meanwhile King's College Chapel (page 112) across the road was taking shape and it's likely that the fine tracery in Great St Mary's was the work of its master mason, John Wastell. The stained glass created by the craftsmen working on the Chapel, however, did not survive the iconoclasm of the 16th and 17th centuries.

Even before King Henry VIII's break with Rome in 1533 over the matter of his divorce from his wife, Katharine of Aragon, which sparked the English Reformation, Martin Luther's reforming ideas had spread widely and Cambridge was becoming a hotbed of Protestantism. It was in Great St Mary's in 1549 that Divine Service was performed in English for the first time.

As the University Church, Great St Mary's attracted some of the most illustrious thinkers, theologians, scholars and philosophers of the time. Of the many reformers who preached here, 35 were burned at the stake as heretics under the reign of the Catholic Queen Mary I between 1553 and 1558.

During the Protestant Queen Elizabeth I's five-day visit to Cambridge in 1564 she came to the church twice to hear scholarly debates and gave her own long speech in fluent Latin.

Whitewashed and divested of its earlier colour, the internal

layout of the church altered over the years to reflect the changes in the style of services as preaching predominated. A huge three-tier pulpit was the central focal point and several galleries were added to accommodate the vast numbers of people who came to hear the lengthy sermons. A major reordering and restoration in the mid-19th century left Great St Mary's much as we see it today.

Tall slender piers and arches with elegant tracery in their spandrels give a sense of height to the nave, drawing the eye beyond the wide chancel arch to the high altar and the 'Majestas'. Carved in wood and gilded, its imagery taken from the Revelation of St John, this shows the robed figure of the resurrected Christ against the cross. Made in 1960 by the British sculptor and wood carver Alan Durst, 'Majestas Christi' is the focus of the church.

The nave roof is original, carved from King Henry VII's gift of oaks. When it was showing signs of decay in the 19th century, a local architect decided to conserve it by building a new roof above and tying the two together. Being so high up, the large carved bosses depicting religious scenes escaped the wrath of the reformers.

Below the roof, the Victorian stained-glass windows in the clerestory are based on verses from the 'Te Deum' hymn of praise. Portraying 60 figures, they take the viewer through the history of Christianity, from Old Testament prophets to the Apostles and martyrs.

There can be few churches of this size with quite so many pews. They fill the nave and the side aisles plus two long galleries above the north and south aisles, and are packed to capacity on special occasions. Installed in 1863, the ends of the nave and aisle pews are carved with ornate poppyheads and depictions of animals, including stags, greyhounds, a lion and a unicorn.

From the same era, the octagonal pulpit has an unusual feature. After complaints that the preacher could not be seen from some parts of the church, a rail was installed so it could be moved into the centre of the chancel arch for university sermons.

Unusually for a parish church, Great St Mary's boasts two fine pipe organs and is one of the few places where double organ concertos can be heard. With its five choirs and the Academy of Great St Mary's symphony orchestra, music here is always of the highest standard.

There are two interesting things to look for outside the church. Near the west door, a disc marks the official centre of the city. It was from this datum point that between 1725 and 1727 Dr William Warren, a Fellow of Trinity Hall, measured three roads out of Cambridge using a 66-foot surveyor's chain. He marked each mile with a stone, which the plaque claims were the first true milestones in Britain since Roman times.

Above the west door, the lovely dial of the church clock is dated 1679. The mechanism is from the late 19th century, but the tune of its chimes, known as the 'Cambridge Quarters', was composed in 1793. It may sound familiar. It was copied in 1859 for the 'Westminster Chimes' of Big Ben on the Houses of Parliament.

Climb the tower's medieval turret staircase (123 steps) for panoramic views of Cambridge, its lovely colleges and far out across the surrounding countryside. For refreshment, walk a short distance up Trinity Street to the former church of St Michael, still consecrated and now the Michaelhouse Centre. Home to an award-winning café wrapped around a chapel, it is used for concerts, art exhibitions and community events.

GUILDFORD CATHEDRAL

An imposing sight atop Stag Hill, Guildford's red-brick Cathedral Church of the Holy Spirit watches over the University of Surrey, the city that spreads out below and the countryside beyond. The only English cathedral to be dedicated to the Holy Spirit, it's also the only Anglican cathedral built to be approached by car, with copious free parking when you arrive. The word 'Welcome', painted in white on the road up the hill, is a nice touch.

When the Diocese of Guildford was created in 1927 the town's parish church was deemed too small to fulfil the role of the Mother Church, so a competition was launched to find an architect 'desirous of erecting a cathedral'. From the 183 submissions, Edward Maufe's Gothic Revival design was chosen.

With the country in severe economic depression and a war looming, the 1930s were hardly a good time to consider such a major building project. Undeterred, planning and fundraising went ahead, boosted when Lord Onslow gave six acres on Stag Hill – so named because it once formed part of royal hunting grounds – for the site of the new cathedral. A cross, made from teak timbers from the battleship HMS *Ganges*, was erected as a marker in 1933. It still stands today, outside the eastern end of the building.

Construction began in 1936 but stopped in 1939 and was boarded up for the duration of the Second World War. In the post-war years, priority was given to the building of houses and many believed the cathedral would never be completed, but the brilliant 'Buy-A-Brick' fundraising campaign launched in 1952 guaranteed its future.

In an early example of crowdfunding, people of all ages came from near and far to buy a brick for two shillings and sixpence (12.5p) and inscribe it with their name. By 1961, about 400,000 bricks had been sold. Ever since, the cathedral has been known as 'the people's cathedral'.

Physically, Guildford Cathedral grew out of the land on which it stands. Almost 780 wooden piles had to be driven up to 50 feet (fifteen metres) into the hillside to secure its foundations, but the soft clay that caused headaches for the contractors also provided the material for many of the 4 million bricks used in its building.

Some of the best British sculptors and artists from the 1950s and 1960s were engaged to work on the cathedral and it is well worth walking around the exterior of the building to experience their creations. Look up to the top of the tower. The fifteen-foot- (four-and-a-half-metre-) high golden angel weather vane, gilded with 22-carat gold leaf, discreetly hides a mobile phone mast.

Standing sentinel, ethereal angels engraved on glass welcome people through the west door entrance. Larger than life-sized, they were created by John Hutton, renowned for his magnificent glass screen of saints and angels in Coventry Cathedral (page 59).

In contrast to the red-brick exterior, inside all is light. In a soaring space of calm simplicity, slim columns rise unimpeded to a great height in the nave and slender arches flow elegantly along the length of the lofty side aisles. Tall lancet windows pierce the walls.

The architect's brief was 'to produce a design definitely of our time, yet in the line of the great English cathedrals, to build anew on tradition'. This Maufe did, combining Gothic tradition with 20th-century construction techniques, including using cast-in-situ concrete for the ceiling vaults.

Photo: Sue Dobson

Light was at the heart of his concept and the colour scheme is predominantly cream and white, with judicious use of blue, decorative gold and touches of red. The brick-built piers of the nave's seven arches are faced with limestone from the Mendip Hills. Another type of limestone, Italian travertine, covers the floor.

The long, slim windows are glazed with handmade translucent glass, 'to simulate the colour of the stone'. While he stipulated that very little stained glass was to be used, in 1939 he commissioned a renowned artist of the time, Moira Forsyth, to create a small rose window above the high altar. It depicts the seven gifts of the Holy Spirit: wisdom, understanding, counsel, fortitude, knowledge, piety and fear of the Lord.

Don't miss John Hutton's superb angel musician, engraved on glass in the St Ursula Porch, where the door reflects Maufe's early links with the Arts and Crafts Movement and five bricks, signed by the Queen and members of the royal family on a visit in 1957, are displayed.

The architect's wife, Prudence, was a designer and a director of Heal's, the department store famed for promoting good modern design. Her input can be seen in the fabrics and furnishings of the cathedral, in the painted panels on the ceiling of the Lady Chapel, but especially in the 1,468 individually designed and hand crafted kneelers in the nave.

The kneeler project began in 1936 with the formation of the Cathedral Broderers' Guild. Volunteers were given her plan for the background – a rectangle divided diagonally into blue and beige halves – and asked to choose a subject for their design that would reflect what they felt it was important to chronicle. The result is three decades of work, involving over 700 crafters, and a social history of the time.

In the north aisle by the Treasury, look for the two maps

showing the cathedral's connections to all the churches in the diocese. When John Clark was a seventeen-year-old schoolboy, he cycled around many of the parishes, sketching the churches and creating a map of them. When he retired he completed an updated, more complicated, version.

Many churches have areas set aside for children but Guildford Cathedral has a dedicated Children's Chapel. Outside, the unique Seeds of Hope Children's Garden, designed to help young people explore loss of all kinds, has bronze sculptures and a maze.

The cathedral was consecrated in 1961, with the building work completed in 1966. The cost was £900,000. Much furnishing, statuary and stained glass have been added over the succeeding years without losing the architect's concept of light and space.

Above the whalebone arches of the main entrance, Charles Gurrey's figures of the Transfigured Christ and men and women whose lives reflect the Holy Spirit, were consecrated in 2004. Within the cathedral, the work of this talented sculptor and carver includes the striking font with its blue bronze bowl.

A bust of Sir Edward Maufe (he was knighted in 1954) stands next to the Lady Chapel. It was placed there because looking west towards the nave was his favourite view.

HEREFORD CATHEDRAL

Compact and friendly, Hereford's pink sandstone Cathedral Church of St Mary the Virgin and St Ethelbert the King is a mix of architecture that reflects a turbulent history –

from the nave's massive Norman piers and elaborately carved chevron-patterned arches, via the Early English Lady Chapel and restored shrine of St Thomas of Hereford, to the modern tapestries by John Piper and a stunning gold corona over the altar.

The traditional date for the founding of Hereford Cathedral is AD 696 and it boasts the shrines of two saints: St Ethelbert, to whom it is dedicated, and St Thomas Cantilupe, Bishop of Hereford from 1275 to 1282.

When in 794, Ethelbert, the young Christian King of the East Angles, travelled west in the hope of marrying the daughter of King Offa of Mercia, he was murdered on the King's orders.

Immediately there were stories of miracles in his name. It was said that when his body was taken to the cathedral to be interred, his severed head fell from the ox-cart and the blind man who retrieved it regained his sight. Another was of how healing waters gushed from springs and a well at stopping points along the way.

Ethelbert's shrine became a focus for vast numbers of pilgrims and in 1020 Bishop Athelstan began rebuilding the Saxon cathedral. It did not stand for long. In 1055, rebel Welsh forces burned it down and most of the relics were destroyed. The saint's head was translated to Westminster and his veneration continued right up to the dissolution of the monasteries. An 8th-century illuminated Gospel Book, known as the Hereford Gospels, survived from this time and remains one of the cathedral's precious treasures.

A modern shrine, created by the noted English iconographer Peter Murphy, stands outside the Lady Chapel on what is thought to be the original site of the saint's tomb. It tells the story of St Ethelbert's life in thirteen brilliantly painted icons.

In the north transept, Peter Murphy's exquisite icon showing the Virgin Mary surrounded by saints associated with Hereford, and two angels holding the Mappa Mundi, adorns the apex of the colourful canopy of the restored tomb shrine of St Thomas Cantilupe.

Known as St Thomas of Hereford, he was an academic, Chancellor of Oxford University, a high-ranking politician and trusted advisor to King Edward I. Excommunicated in 1282 after a dispute with the Archbishop of Canterbury, he travelled to Rome to plead his cause with the Pope and died while in Italy. His bones were returned to Hereford for burial in his cathedral.

With his tomb a site of pilgrimage that reached cult proportions, the number of miracles of healing was said to be second only to those associated with the shrine of Archbishop Thomas Becket at Canterbury (page 37). Over 400 were certified for his canonisation in 1320. Income from the offerings of pilgrims funded great building improvements, notably the elegant central tower with its distinctive 'ballflower' decoration.

Consecrated in 1142, Hereford was one of the last English cathedrals to be rebuilt by the Normans following the Conquest. Its sturdy Romanesque pillars lining the nave lead the eye to the stunning corona above the central altar under the tower.

Installed in 1992, it was designed by the acclaimed British silversmith Simon Beer and holds fourteen candles, which represent the fourteen deaneries in the diocese. Symbolising Christ's Crown of Thorns and his Crown of Glory, its design echoes the chevron patterning in the nave arches.

The south transept retains early Norman work. John Piper's lovely tapestries hang within three arches of its blind arcading on the east wall. Woven in Namibia, they

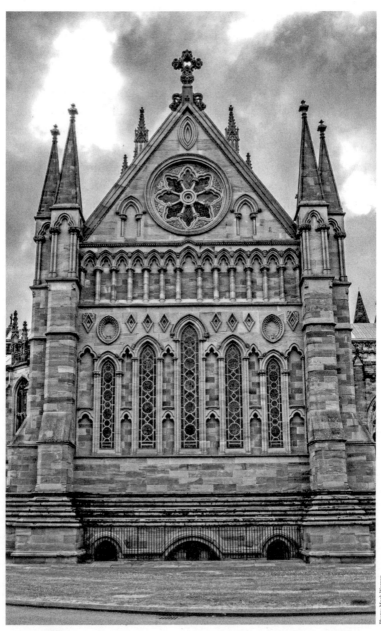

Photo: Mark Warren

were placed there in 1976 for the 1,300th anniversary of the diocese. On the opposite wall there's a 16th-century triptych of the Adoration of the Magi and in one corner, a modern icon of St Anne is a reminder that an altar dedicated to the saint stood in the transept during much of the Middle Ages.

The north transept is entirely different. Its east side, more French than English, was a sophisticated addition by the Savoyard Bishop Aigueblanche in the mid-13th century. Chaplain to King Henry III's teenage queen, Eleanor of Provence, he was more interested in the latest fashion in architecture at Westminster Abbey than local concerns, which his towering, elaborately carved tomb reflects.

The 14th-century stalls in the quire still have their carved misericords, though the pew ends were part of the Victorian restoration, which included the ornately patterned tile floor and the addition of a jewelled metal screen. This was removed in 1967 and can be seen, splendidly restored, in the Victoria and Albert Museum in London.

In the north quire aisle, don't miss the little chantry chapel of Bishop John Stanbury, confessor to King Henry VI. Dating from around 1350 and roofed with fan vaulting, it has very fine stone carving and brilliant Arts and Crafts stained-glass windows showing scenes from the bishop's life and his enthronement in the cathedral.

The spacious, light and lovely Lady Chapel (1220–30) is considered among the finest expressions of Early English architecture. On one side is the gloriously painted Audley Chapel screen, a reminder of how colourful cathedrals were before the Reformation.

Step inside the chapel to see the powerful windows by renowned British stained-glass artist Tom Denny. Installed in 2007, they celebrate the 17th-century Herefordshire writer and poet, Thomas Traherne.

For much of its history, the 13th-century crypt below the Lady Chapel, now reserved as a quiet chapel, was used as a charnel house for bones dug up in the cathedral close.

While Hereford suffered during the Reformation, the Civil War of the 1640s wrought greater destruction. Never properly restored, disaster struck on Easter Monday 1786, when the entire west front collapsed, taking with it several bays of the nave.

The famous but chaotic architect, Thomas Wyatt, rebuilt it, not to everyone's approval. With the building's fabric continuing to deteriorate into the 19th century, it was left to the Victorians to come to the rescue. A major restoration project spanned the years from 1841 to 1863, when the cathedral reopened for worship.

John Oldrid Scott replaced Wyatt's west front facade in 1908, decorating it with statues of saints and personages associated with Hereford. At night, architectural lighting shows it to best effect.

The cathedral's greatest treasures are the Mappa Mundi and extensive Chained Library, both displayed along with an interpretative exhibition in the award-winning purpose-built New Library building adjoining the cloisters.

Drawn on a single sheet of vellum and depicting the known world in the late 13th century from a Christian perspective, the extraordinary Mappa Mundi, the largest map known to have survived from the Middle Ages, is full of fascinating detail and imagery.

The earth is round, Jerusalem is at the centre and east at the top, with Christ enthroned in Majesty above his creation. The map depicts 420 cities and towns, fifteen biblical events, 33 plants, animals, birds and strange creatures, 32 images of the peoples of the world and eight pictures from classical mythology. Biblical landmarks include the Garden of Eden, Noah's Ark and the Tower of Babel.

Over 220 medieval manuscript books, together with around 1,500 books dating from the year 800 through to the early 19th century, are held in Hereford's Chained Library. It's the world's largest surviving chained library, with its volumes displayed on early 17th-century shelves. The building also contains the cathedral's archive collection, which includes the 1217 revision of the Magna Carta, plus a large collection of music manuscripts.

Before you leave the Cathedral Close, look for the statue of Sir Edward Elgar and his bicycle. Although usually associated with Worcester, Elgar lived in Hereford for several years and the charming statue is a delightful tribute to the much-loved British composer.

HOLY TRINITY CHURCH, STRATFORD-UPON-AVON

Affectionately known as 'Shakespeare's church', Holy Trinity is where the Bard was baptised, where he worshipped and where he and his wife Anne are buried.

On the banks of the River Avon, it's a lovely old church dating from 1210, although there's been a place of worship on the site since a Saxon monastery was founded there in the early 8th century. With around a quarter of a million visitors a year, it is surely the most visited parish church in the land.

The peaceful approach is through an avenue of lime trees, said to represent the twelve tribes of Israel and the twelve Apostles. Entrance to the church is via the two-storey 15th-century porch, which has its original tracery and stone vault. A small door inset into the massive oak doors bears a sanctuary knocker, which a fugitive could grasp and be offered 37 days of safety before facing trial.

The transept and the nave pillars at the crossing that support the tower are the oldest parts of the church and date back to 1210. There are faint remnants of pre-Reformation wall painting on a pillar in the crossing. The south aisle was added in the 1300s and the chancel in the late 1400s.

From the nave you can see that the chancel is set at a slight angle. Known as a 'weeping chancel' it represents the drooping head of the crucified Christ and is often seen in medieval churches, including the University Church in Oxford (page 228).

It seems that William Shakespeare had bought the right to be buried in the chancel of the church and that his family inherited it. His wife Anne Hathaway, daughter Susanna, son-in-law Dr John Hall and Thomas Nash, the first husband of his only granddaughter Elizabeth, are buried alongside him.

Their graves are marked by simple stone slabs and as was the way in those times, their bodies were buried directly into the earth. The memorial to William Shakespeare on the wall was made a few years after his death, but still during Anne's lifetime, so the bust is considered to be a good likeness.

There was a charnel house attached to the church in Shakespeare's time, where the bones of those buried in the churchyard were placed when it was necessary to make room for more interments. Its entrance door was very close to his own burial place before the altar, which he didn't like at all, hence the inscription, which tradition says he wrote himself: 'Good frend for Jesus sake forbeare, To dig the dust encloased heare; Blest be ye man yt spare thes stones, And curst be he yt moves my bones.'

Nearby are copies of register entries for Shakespeare's

Photo: DeFacto

baptism and burial and the original font in which he was baptised. The chained King James Bible, a first edition from 1611, would have been read from during his lifetime.

The stone slab that sits atop the Victorian altar predates King Henry VIII's Reformation. It had been hidden during the years of destruction when much of the church's statuary and treasure was lost, and was rediscovered three centuries later, buried underneath the floor.

Do look at the misericords in the quire stalls, a wonderful collection of carvings depicting the sacred and secular. They span everything from angels to mythical beasts and a woman beating up her husband.

The screen that divides the crossing from the chancel is a fine example of 15th-century carving. The original 14th-century rood screen now seals off the north transept but is rather hidden by storyboards that explain Shakespeare's life and connections with the church.

There's a small chapel dedicated to St Peter in the south transept where the stained-glass window, installed in 1896, was 'The Gift of America to Shakespeare's Church'.

In 1331 when John de Stratford was Bishop of Winchester (he went on to be Archbishop of Canterbury and Chancellor of England), he founded and endowed a chantry chapel dedicated to St Thomas of Canterbury in the south aisle, which he enlarged and rebuilt for the purpose.

He endowed the chantry with lands and in 1352 an impressive house was built for the priests by his nephew, Ralph de Stratford, Bishop of London. The house was known as a college and the church became The Collegiate Church of the Holy and Undivided Trinity, a title it still holds.

The building went into private hands after chantries were abolished under King Henry VIII. One of its owners was John Combe, a friend of Shakespeare, also buried in the chancel of the church. It was demolished in 1799 but is remembered in local street names.

During the period 1480 to 1520 the college was responsible for the complete rebuilding of the nave with its elegantly Perpendicular clerestories, the tower, the north porch and the enlargement of the chancel to include the quire stalls and its misericords.

The splendid Clopton Chapel in the north aisle is packed with the elaborate tombs of the wealthy and politically-important 15th- and 16th-century Clopton family. Look carefully at the stained-glass window. The top lights are pre-Reformation in origin, the lower lights with the figures of Faith, Hope and Charity in much brighter colours, are late Victorian.

Stained glass, installed between 1897 and 1909, fills every window in the nave and chancel, and it's all by nationally acclaimed designers of that period. With strong colours and intricate detail, they tell many stories.

Suitably for 'Shakespeare's Church' there's a Poets Window (located above the shop). It depicts Cædmon, the earliest known English poet who lived at Whitby (page 241) in the 7th century; Geoffrey Chaucer, considered to be the father of English poetry, best known as the author of *The Canterbury Tales*; and John Milton, whose *Paradise Lost* has been deemed the greatest epic poem in the English language.

Notice the kneelers in the pews. The imagery in the 33 different designs is based on the *Benedicite* canticle used in Morning Prayer. There are 364 and it took a team of around 40 volunteers over twenty years to complete them.

KING'S COLLEGE CHAPEL, CAMBRIDGE

Painted by Turner and Canaletto, praised in verse by William Wordsworth, King's College Chapel is a gem in a city of standout architecture. Begun in 1446, it took nearly 100 years to build, involving five successive kings, four master masons and countless skilled craftsmen.

Entering through the north porch you are immediately immersed in the spacious vastness of the Chapel. The long, exquisitely beautiful fan vaulting – that intricate lacework of stone that was a uniquely English contribution to Gothic architecture – seems to float above the spectacular stained-glass windows. Measuring 289 feet (88.5 metres) in length, it is 40 feet (12.6 metres) wide and was completed in a mere three years, from 1512 to 1515.

The finely sculpted side walls are decorated with heraldic carvings and Tudor symbols, the boldest being the Tudor rose. Incorporating the red rose of the triumphant House of Lancaster and the white rose of the House of York, it's the symbol of the union of Henry VII and Elizabeth of York, the marriage that brought together the two factions in the civil war that became known as the Wars of the Roses.

Look too for the lattice grille portcullis and greyhound, emblems of the Beaufort family, Lady Margaret Beaufort being King Henry VII's mother; the Welsh dragon of Henry VII's father's family and the fleur de lys, a reminder that English kings had also been kings of France. The Royal Arms of King Henry VII appear frequently. Worshippers would have been left in no doubt of the power and importance of the Tudors.

Side chapels tuck in alongside, their entrance stone steps

worn by the tread of centuries, their windows containing fragments of medieval glass. Don't miss the 16th-century triptych of scenes from Christ's early life in the Founder's Chapel.

Ahead, the triumphal, heavily carved and decorated quire screen in dark English oak was the gift of King Henry VIII. A superb example of Tudor woodwork, it is filled with stylised flowers, masks, strange creatures and heraldic badges, all studded with the king's initials (HR, Henricus Rex) and those of his second queen, Anne Boleyn (AR, Anna Regina). In places their initials are intertwined, bound up in a lovers' knot. As they were married in 1533 and Anne was executed three years later, this boldly romantic declaration gives a clear indication of the period the screen must have been designed and installed. Above it, angels trumpet from atop the gilded pipes of the great organ.

A splendid double-sided and beautifully engraved brass lectern greets you as you enter the quire. The gift of Robert Hacumblen, Provost of King's College in the early 16th century and much involved with the building of the Chapel, it is topped with a statuette of the chapel's founder, King Henry VI, bearing an orb and sceptre.

The long rows of quire stalls were probably installed around the same time as the screen but their canopies and the heraldic carved panels behind them date from the 17th century. The magnificent painting of *The Adoration of the Magi* by Sir Peter Paul Rubens is the focal point of the high altar. The quire was the first part of the chapel to be built and, lacking the Tudor bombast of the antechapel, reflects King Henry VI's plan for simplicity.

When King Henry VI established King's College in 1441, his stated wish was for a choir to provide the music for the offices and celebrations in his new chapel. Today

Photo: Delphine Ménard

King's College Choir is famed worldwide, known especially for 'A Festival of Nine Lessons and Carols', broadcast live on Christmas Eve, and for their international tours and recordings. During term time the choir, comprising sixteen boy choristers aged between nine and thirteen years, and fourteen male undergraduates, sing daily chapel services. To hear Evensong sung here is a memorable experience, well worth queuing up for.

King's College Chapel is blessed with 26 vast windows, twelve on each side flanked by an east and a west window. Lit by sunshine, their jewel-like colours bathe the interior with warmth. The work of Flemish glaziers, each window demands time to simply stand and stare. The glass is original, a rare survival of the Reformation, making it the finest collection of 16th-century stained glass in England.

Packed with detailed figures the windows depict scenes from the Old and New Testaments, many emphasising events that link the two by prefiguring or symbolising the coming and life of Christ. The east window gives the narrative of the Passion and Crucifixion. They were all completed between 1515 and 1547, except the Great West Window, which shows the Last Judgement and dates from the mid-19th century.

The Chapel is one of the finest and most complete late Perpendicular Gothic buildings in Britain, constructed in three separate phases between 1446 and 1515, a tumultuous period in England's history that spanned the Wars of the Roses (1455–87). Installing the stained-glass windows took a further 30 years.

King Henry VI, known for his piety and religious devotion, drew up a design for the chapel in 1448 and detailed how it was to be built, decorated and funded. It was to be 'without equal in size and beauty', a simple, grand statement, unencumbered by superfluous decorative details.

The simple rectangular ground plan is very much as he stipulated, but it's unlikely that he would have approved of some of the decoration that was to come.

After his murder in the Tower of London in 1471, building work continued sporadically under King Edward IV and more intensely under King Richard III. By the time of Richard's death at the Battle of Bosworth in 1485, the first five bays of the Chapel were already in use.

Two Tudor kings completed and made their mark on this glorious work of art and craftsmanship. Building work began again in earnest in 1508 under King Henry VII, who sent some of the money to pay for it in the strong wooden chest bound with iron that's now on display in the Chapel Exhibition. He left generous funds in his will to cover the cost of the stonework, including master mason John Wastell's superb fan vault, and some of the glazing. Finally his son, King Henry VIII, made his contribution with the magnificent carved oak quire screen, the quire stalls and the immense glass windows.

An excellent exhibition in the north side chapels charts the construction stages and methods, shows how the glass was made, makes sense of the period and puts everything into context.

LICHFIELD CATHEDRAL

One of the glories of Early English architecture, the Cathedral Church of St Mary and St Chad was built during the 13th and early 14th centuries on the site of earlier Saxon and Norman churches. Surrounded by a grassy close and edged by a peaceful lake, it is the only medieval cathedral in Britain with three spires (known locally as 'The Ladies of the Vale'). In the sunshine, its red sandstone, mottled black by age and the elements, glows with welcoming warmth.

Tiers of life-sized statues, 113 in all, give the west front a powerful presence. Here beneath Christ in Glory are angels and archangels, saints and martyrs, patriarchs, prophets, Apostles and disciples, bishops, kings, scientists and theologians, a storyboard of biblical characters and English social history. Walk around the building and you'll find 40 more perched on buttresses, around doors and in arcading. They are mainly Victorian replacements and include a statue of Queen Victoria, sculpted by her daughter, Princess Louise.

In soft pink-grey sandstone, the 13th-century nave is a masterpiece of Gothic symmetry, its pointed arches and high ceiling vaulting leading the eye eastwards to the glorious windows of the Lady Chapel.

Suspended above the nave altar, the life-sized icon of Christ Crucified, Risen and Lord of All was created in 2018 by students and tutors from the Bethlehem Icon Centre and School. It followed on from their first visit to Lichfield in 2016 when they wrote two icons depicting the Archangel Gabriel and the Virgin Mary, together known as The Lichfield Annunciation. These are placed on nave pillars, a meditative focus at services.

The impressive quire, which is a similar length to the nave, is introduced at the crossing by a magnificent wrought metalwork screen. A gem of High Victorian craftsmanship, its design echoes that of the high altar, which it seems to frame. Across the top, gilded musical angels enthusiastically trumpet their praise.

At the east end of the cathedral, the glorious Lady Chapel was completed around 1330 in the Decorated Gothic style. It was financed by Bishop de Langton, who was also Treasurer of England in the reign of King Edward I. Langton transformed the cathedral into his personal citadel, fortifying it with high crenellated walls and building an immense, castle-like bishop's palace.

The windows, soaring to a height of 36 feet (eleven metres) and containing some of the finest medieval Flemish painted glass in existence, are the highlight and dominating feature of the Lady Chapel. Installed in 1803 they date from the 1530s and were rescued from Herkenrode Abbey in Belgium, dissolved during the Napoleonic Wars. A £3.7 million, five-year restoration project has revealed their true vibrant colours and extraordinary detail.

The late 19th-century altarpiece, a triptych in blue and gold, comes from Oberammergau. Richly carved and gilded, the central panel depicts the Nativity (one of the three kings wears a Tyrolean hat) and associated scenes.

Bishop de Langton spent the astonishing sum of £2,000 on a sumptuous shrine for the bones of St Chad. Cast in gold and richly bejewelled, in medieval times this was on display in the Lady Chapel. An icon now marks the spot. Nearby, up some stairs, is St Chad's Head Chapel, where the skull of the saint was kept.

St Chad was the Anglo-Saxon missionary bishop of Mercia who founded a small monastery and church at Lichfield, making it the centre of a diocese that stretched from the Welsh border to the North Sea and from Northumberland to the River Thames. His brother, St Cedd, became Bishop of the East Saxons in 654 and is one of the saints to whom Chelmsford Cathedral (page 43) is dedicated.

Although he was the Bishop of Lichfield for less than three years, from 669 until his death from the plague in 672, in that short time he made many converts to Christianity.

Photo: Michael D Beckwith

Known for his humility and holiness, his shrine quickly became a place of pilgrimage and many reports of healing were recorded. His relics were venerated here right up to the Reformation, when the cathedral was stripped of its riches.

Lichfield suffered more than any other cathedral during the English Civil War. Turned into a garrison, between 1643 and 1646 it was occupied by forces on both sides, batting between the Royalists and the Parliamentary forces that finally prevailed and occupied the building for the next fourteen years.

Cannon fire destroyed the tall central spire, causing devastating damage as it fell; all the stained glass was smashed, altars desecrated, arcading and statues defaced and lead stripped from the roof in an orgy of ransacking, looting and vandalism.

By the time of the Restoration of the monarchy to the throne in 1660, there wasn't too much left of Lichfield's once-great cathedral. Yet under the guiding hand of Bishop John Hacket (and monetary support from King Charles II) rebuilding commenced. In seven years the roofs and towers had been replaced and the cathedral was rededicated on Christmas Eve, 1669 – a story strikingly depicted in a south aisle window.

The first services after the war were held in the 13th-century chapter house, the only part of the building with a roof. Situated off the north transept it is reached via a very rare example of a pedilavium, used for the washing of feet on Maundy Thursday.

It is the only two-storey chapter house in Britain and the only one shaped liked a stretched octagon. Here, under vaults flowing from a central pillar, are displayed some of the cathedral's greatest treasures: the 8th-century illuminated St Chad Gospels and the Saxon Lichfield Angel, a carved limestone panel thought to be part of a tomb chest, discovered in 2003 during excavations in the nave.

Renovations in the 17th and 18th centuries were not all good, and the Victorian architect, Sir George Gilbert Scott, righted many wrongs. Scott took charge in 1857 and work continued after his death in 1878 under his son, John Oldrid Scott. Considered some of his best work, much of the beautiful cathedral we see today is due to Scott's restoration.

Where possible he retained the medieval work; where he could not, he imitated it. Fragments found during the building work informed the design of the stalls in the quire and the very fine floor tiles, made by Minton Hollins & Co.. He commissioned the finest makers of stained glass for the windows and the best sculptors, metalworkers and craftspeople of the period. By 1908 the cathedral was back to the form Scott believed it would have taken in the Middle Ages.

LINCOLN CATHEDRAL

Crowning the city, its three vast towers visible for miles, Lincoln's hilltop Cathedral Church of the Blessed Virgin Mary is one of the finest medieval buildings in Europe. It is huge – in terms of floor area, among English cathedrals only St Paul's in London (page 193) and York Minster (page 258) are bigger – and it presents a dramatic and elegant face to the world.

The 14th-century towers, delicate, lacy and topped with sky-piercing pinnacles, rise up behind the west front's 13th-century screen with its rows of Norman niches, Early Gothic blind arcading and handsome Norman doors.

The towers today are an impressive height, but when the central tower collapsed in 1237 its replacement was topped with a spire, reputedly making Lincoln's cathedral the tallest man-made structure in the world, topping even Egypt's Great Pyramid at Giza. It held that record for 238 years, until the 525-foot (160-metre) spire blew down in a raging storm in 1548 and wasn't replaced.

William the Conqueror ordered a cathedral to be built on the hill in Lincoln, sited next to his castle for security, and sent Bishop Remigius to supervise it. Constructed of locally quarried Lincolnshire limestone and consecrated in 1092, it commanded a vast diocese that stretched from the Humber estuary in the north to the River Thames in the south, spanning nine counties and encompassing several notable and wealthy monasteries.

After a devastating earthquake in 1185, Hugh of Avalon, a Carthusian monk of character, began the rebuilding of the cathedral, greatly enlarging it in the Early Gothic style, incorporating pointed arches, ribbed vaults, lancet windows and flying buttresses. Consecrated Bishop of Lincoln in 1186, he died in 1200 and was canonised in 1220 – in good time for the completion of the new cathedral, which saw pilgrims flocking to his shrine.

The long nave is soaring and lyrical, a space of beauty and light – especially when sunshine pours through the fine Victorian stained glass and dapples the limestone floor and piers with patterns of rich colour. Graceful arched stone ribs draw the eye heavenwards.

At the nave's end, the elaborate quire screen is a tour de force of early 14th-century carving, alive with beasts, heads and fantasy creatures among leaves and flowers.

The Bishop's Eye floods the transept with light from on high. A magnificent circular rose window of precious medieval stained glass, its graceful tracery of leaves encases the glass with softly curving lines. Facing it on the north side, the earlier (13th-century) Dean's Eye rose window has four circles surrounded by sixteen smaller ones, with some of its original Last Judgement narrative still discernible.

Ornate 13th-century doorways lead to the quire aisles – look for dragons hiding behind foliage and the sword-bearing men seeking them out – and bring you towards a forest of exquisite wood and stone carving of heart-stopping delicacy.

The angels, carved on the quire desks around 1370, play harps, pipes and a drum; etched in gold above the canopied and pinnacled quire stalls with their secretive misericords are the first lines of psalms each canon was appointed to read.

The Treasury is located in the north side quire aisle. It was the first open Treasury in an English cathedral and as well as Lincoln's own silverware it contains other sacred pieces from churches around the diocese. The highlight is a medieval chalice hallmarked 1489.

Behind the high altar, the Gothic Angel Choir has a feast of stone carving and impressive stained-glass windows. It was created to hold the shrine of St Hugh, whose following was so large that the cathedral had to be extended 80 years after his death to accommodate all the pilgrims. King Edward I and Queen Eleanor were among the great and the good that were there to see his body translated to the site prepared for him.

The infamous Lincoln imp has his place here among the host of presiding angels. The legend goes that the mischievous imp caused mayhem in the cathedral and when he started throwing rocks at the angels they turned him to stone. He may be quite difficult to spot high up in his spandrel, but his image has long been a symbol of the city.

The tomb of King Edward I's beloved wife Eleanor of

Photo: Lee Haywood

Castile, who died near Lincoln in 1290, contains the viscera from her embalmed body, which was borne with great ceremony to London. The King decreed that a monument should be erected at each of the twelve towns where the funeral procession stopped overnight on its journey south. Being topped by tall crosses, they became known as 'Eleanor Crosses'.

Eleanor's Lincoln tomb, a replica of that in Westminster Abbey, was badly damaged in the English Civil War by Oliver Cromwell's forces during their siege of Lincoln in 1644 and the effigy seen above the stone chest is a 19th-century copy.

Among the many small chapels, some very poignant like the Airmen's Chapel that especially remembers the men of Bomber Command who flew from nearby airfields in the Second World War, the Russell Chantry stands out for its murals painted by Bloomsbury Group member Duncan Grant in the 1950s.

Although never a monastic foundation, the cathedral has a fan-vaulted chapter house (1220) and relatively small but attractive cloisters (1295) with Gothic arches and a wooden ceiling. King Edward I conducted meetings of Parliament in the chapter house on three occasions and the stained-glass windows tell of events in the cathedral's history.

Above the cloisters, a thousand years of history are recorded in manuscripts and books. The 15th-century Medieval Library still retains many of its chained books and holds among its riches a 10th-century copy of homilies by the historian the Venerable Bede, hand painted atlases and a manuscript of Chaucer's *The Canterbury Tales*. The Wren Library, designed in 1674 by Sir Christopher Wren, the architect of St Paul's Cathedral (page 193), is a beautiful setting for a fascinating collection of early printed books, including 100 printed before 1501. The libraries are open to the public between April and October.

For centuries it was where one of the only four surviving copies of Magna Carta, signed by King John in 1215, was held. The then Bishop of Lincoln, Hugh of Wells, was one of those present for the sealing at Runnymede. It is now on permanent loan to nearby Lincoln Castle, but a facsimile copy can be seen near the cloisters.

The Victorian writer John Ruskin wrote: 'I have always held that the cathedral of Lincoln is out and out the most precious piece of architecture in the British Isles.' In its shadow, over Minster Yard, is the Medieval Bishop's Palace while across the square William the Conqueror's castle, dating from 1068, affords splendid views over the lower town and surrounding countryside.

LLANDAFF CATHEDRAL

The seat of the Archbishop of Wales, Llandaff's Cathedral Church of Saints Peter and Paul, with Saints Dyfrig, Teilo and Euddogwy, stands on the site of a 6th-century monastery founded by the Celtic saints to whom it is dedicated. Between the River Taff and a tranquil conservation area on the edge of Cardiff, this was one of the earliest Christian sites in Britain.

The cathedral's fragmented and dramatic history is revealed in its architecture. Begun in 1120 under the Norman Bishop Urban, here you'll find Romanesque and Gothic arches, Early English lancet windows, Pre-Raphaelite stained glass and 20th-century modernism.

The west front sets the scene: its centre section dates from 1220; the north tower, a gift from Jasper Tudor, uncle of King Henry VII, dates from 1485, while the south tower with its pencil-sharpened spire and statuary is Victorian, completed in 1869.

Step through the 13th-century west doorway with its strange dipping pendant and enter the nave. Here, spanning the bays of Gothic arches, Sir Jacob Epstein's 1950s aluminium sculpture of Christ in Majesty towers above a sweeping, double wishbone concrete arch. This divides the nave from the quire without breaking the vista of the entire length of the cathedral, right through to Geoffrey Webb's beautifully coloured Tree of Jesse Window in the Lady Chapel at the east end.

Known as 'The Majestas', Epstein's stunning sixteen-foot- (4.9-metre-) tall sculpture of the risen Christ is mounted on a concrete cylinder that was built to encase part of the organ. This is surrounded by 64 small gilded Pre-Raphaelite figures depicting winged angels with musical instruments and the seated forms of characters from the Old Testament. It is just one of the innovations at Llandaff that caused consternation at the time but have since proved to be highly appreciated features.

Over the centuries much change has been wrought to the fabric of the building but apart from the decoration, the lovely light Lady Chapel has remained largely undisturbed since it was built around 1280.

It was during the first half of the 20th century that the renowned stained-glass artist, Geoffrey Fuller Webb, designed the windows and stencilled patterns over the walls. The main window shows the Tree of Jesse, the others show scenes from the life of the Virgin Mary, whose image he modelled on his daughter.

The 15th-century stonework of the reredos behind the altar is mainly original. It was discovered in a builders' yard and restored to its rightful place in 1935. The niches had remained empty since they were stripped of their statues during the Reformation, but in 1954 they were coloured and filled with gilded panels. Against a red background, each of the twelve panels depicts a wild flower named in Welsh in honour of the Virgin Mary, whose statue in white Portland stone is set in the centre of the screen. Ancient and modern meld beautifully in the Lady Chapel, as it does elsewhere in the building.

At times the damage to the cathedral had been so extensive that it seemed beyond repair. It remained neglected for 300 years after the forces of Owain Glyndwr had wrecked it during the Welsh Rebellion of 1400 and the Parliamentarian troops had done their worst during the English Civil War in the 17th century. After severe storm damage a century later, when the roof collapsed, only the Lady Chapel was left in any shape for services to be held.

Work began on a new cathedral in 1734. Leaving the western part in ruins, Bath architect John Wood the Elder's design for the eastern portion was described as 'an Italianate temple'. It was not appreciated and his work disappeared when the next restructuring took place in 1841. This revealed that Wood had not torn down ancient remains but covered them up, hiding them behind walls.

Thus was discovered the beautifully carved Norman arch that now frames the high altar. It dates back to the cathedral begun by Bishop Urban, where it was the chancel arch, and has five bands of carving patterned with medallions enclosing flowers. Above the 'Urban arch' is John Piper's vibrant 1959 window depicting three disciples walking with Jesus to Emmaus.

Between 1843 and 1869 much of the restoration was completed by local architect John Pritchard, who favoured the neo-Gothic style. It was through his partnership with

Photo: Michael D Beckwith

London architect John Pollard Seddon that members of the Pre-Raphaelite Brotherhood of artists, among them William Morris, Edward Burne-Jones and Ford Maddox Brown, were commissioned to create five beautiful stained-glass windows. Daniel Gabriel Rossetti painted the Seed of David triptych in the Illtyd Chapel.

Rossetti used several of the Brotherhood members and their friends as models for the figures depicted in the three panels, including William Morris for the head of King David and Morris' wife Jane Burden for the Virgin Mary. He painted it as the reredos for the high altar but the lighting there was not ideal.

Fortunately it was removed for safekeeping before the cathedral was severely damaged by a parachute mine in 1941, when the roof was blown off the nave and 13th-century chapter house, windows were shattered and general devastation wrought to much of the fabric. Among Britain's Anglican cathedrals, only Coventry (page 59) suffered more war damage than that inflicted on Llandaff.

After the war the triptych found a new, better lit, home in the Illtyd Chapel. A memorial to the 53rd Welsh (Infantry) Division and furnished in the style of 18th-century Dutch churches, it recognises the part played by the Division in the liberation of Holland in 1944.

Ecclesiastical architect George Pace of York oversaw the post-war reconstruction of the cathedral, which was finally completed in 1960. Among his many legacies are the striking wishbone arch and gilded black pine pulpit, the Processional Way linking the Prebendal House with the cathedral and the creation of four chapels in the north and south aisles, all named after Celtic saints.

St Teilo's Chapel includes a reliquary mounted on Art Nouveau silver and holding the reputed skull of St Teilo, whose gilded 13th-century tomb is near the high altar. Fallen airmen are remembered in the small chapel dedicated to St Euddogwy, in particular those of 614 (Auxiliary) Squadron RAF.

Saints Teilo, Tydfil and Elfan are depicted in a window in the Dyfrig Chapel, where a series of six pottery panels designed by Edward Burne-Jones show Pre-Raphaelite angels holding roundels illustrating the Six Days of Creation.

The David or Welch Regimental Chapel is George Pace's extension to the cathedral. Entered through a Romanesque doorway off the north aisle, it is a peaceful space in which to remember those killed in many wars. The outer walls are faced with traditional Taff River-washed pebbles, as are the walls of the Processional Way with its arcade of pointed arches reminiscent of ancient churches in the Vale of Glamorgan.

Outside above the windows, look for the long panels filled with the carved heads of sovereigns from Richard III to Elizabeth II. To the west of the chapter house, seek out Pace's illustrated phases of the building over the centuries.

A story of construction, destruction and reconstruction, Llandaff Cathedral has survived the ravages of Owain Glyndwr, the Reformation, Oliver Cromwell's Parliamentarian troops, the great storms of the 18th century and the Cardiff Blitz of the Second World War, to emerge and remain a much-loved place of worship.

MALMESBURY ABBEY

The sturdy Norman pillars that march down the aisle of Malmesbury Abbey are brought to an abrupt halt, stopped in their tracks by a vast, white-painted wall.

The great Abbey was drastically reduced in size even before the Reformation when the magnificent spire, which was even taller than that on Salisbury Cathedral (page 197), collapsed in the late 15th century, taking the crossing tower with it. The damage was so profound – 116 feet (35 metres) of nave and its wide transept were reduced to rubble – that the wall was erected to save the remains of the building. A hundred years later the west tower came crashing down, demolishing three bays of the nave.

Dedicated to St Peter and St Paul, the Abbey we visit today is about a third of its original size, but it still presents an imposing sight on its hill just off Malmesbury's High Street. It's an intriguing mix of ruins and active parish church, that's also a much-loved venue for concerts and theatrical productions.

It was on this site that Maildulph, an Irish monk, established a hermitage in the 7th century and founded a school for local boys. It is said that one of his pupils was St Aldhelm, a relative of King Ine of Wessex, who went on to be a great scholar, poet, traveller and advisor to royalty.

- In 676 he was made the first Abbot at Malmesbury, where he oversaw the construction of a complex of stone churches in what is now the Abbey's graveyard, and then became the first Bishop of Sherborne. On his death in 709, his body was returned to Malmesbury for burial. St Aldhelm's Chapel, a place for quiet prayer, is at the far end of the south aisle.

The present Abbey dates from 1180 and was added to in the following 200 years. The truncated, late Norman nave is still splendid, with cylindrical piers, scalloped capitals and beady-eyed grotesques and dragons above the slightly pointed arches.

Up on the next level, the triforium has a gallery of smaller arches and the Benedictine monks would have walked along its passage on their way to their many and frequent daily services.

There's an oddity on the nave's south side: the box-like structure, added in the 13th century, is a 'watching loft'. From here a monk could keep a keen eye on the pilgrims passing below. They came in large numbers, often from a great distance, to see and be close to the holy relics in the church.

High above, the soaring lierne vault has a collection of ceiling bosses, repainted in their original colours. There's foliage and a Green Man, but who the faces represent has been lost in the mists of time. A trolley mirror helpfully brings them, and high points of the architecture, into focus.

From the 11th to the 13th century the monastery and its abbey were noted throughout Europe as an important seat of learning, with a famous library and scriptorium. The four volumes of a 15th-century Bible on display in the church are a reminder of the beauty of illustrated manuscripts and the awe-inspiring skill of their artists.

The Bible was written in Latin on vellum in a Belgian monastery in 1447. The monks used handmade tools, writing with goose feather quills, creating their own inks from natural substances. Known as a 'Refectory Bible' it was intended to be read aloud to the monks while they ate.

The tomb of King Athelstan stands in the north aisle. A grandson of Alfred the Great, a wily politician and military leader, he was crowned King of Wessex in 925. By 927 he had created the kingdom of all England, then ten years later defeated the Scots, Danes, Norse and Irish at the bloody Battle of Brunanburh. The inscription on his coins read 'ruler of the whole of Britain'.

Athelstan was a great benefactor of the abbey, granting it lands and privileges, and when he died in Gloucester in 939 his body was brought to Malmesbury for burial. His

Photo: Ethan Doyle White

bones lie somewhere on the abbey site, for he was buried under a long lost tower, and the tomb you see is actually a 14th-century memorial.

Against the wall alongside it, glass cabinets display some of the abbey's treasures, including a silver penny minted in Malmesbury during William the Conqueror's reign, a pre-Civil War chalice and a first English edition of a Bible commentary by Martin Luther.

A stained-glass window depicting a quartet of early monks from the abbey's history is tucked away above the crèche in the restored west end. There's the Irish Maildulph bearing a book of learning and next to him is Eilmer, shown holding the wings that sent him into history as 'the flying monk'.

In around 1010, Eilmer, who was skilled in mathematics and astrology, made a daring attempt at flight. He made himself wings and jumped from the top of the tower. That he broke his legs as he crash-landed he attributed to failing to make himself a tail.

Next to a suitably impressive St Aldhelm, complete with bishop's crozier and halo is the renowned historian William of Malmesbury (c1095–1143). Educated in the monastery, William spent most of his life there as monk, librarian and precentor. Known for his attention to detail and accuracy, his use of documentary evidence and eyewitness accounts, his work has been an invaluable source of knowledge for historians down the centuries.

Abbot Richard Selwyn surrendered Malmesbury Abbey to King Henry VIII's commissioners in 1539. It was sold, together with all its considerable lands and property, to a rich merchant and clothier, William Stumpe, who returned what was left of the abbey church to the town for use as its parish church, which it remains to this day.

Its highlight and greatest treasure is the magnificent,

late-12th-century, multi-arched Norman porch. Intensely decorated with stone carvings that would originally have been brightly coloured, here you get biblical stories from the Creation to the Life of Christ.

The monumental carvings on the walls of the inner porch show the Apostles at Pentecost, six seated on each side, dressed in flowing robes and with an angel in flight overhead. A tympanum of Christ in Majesty, seated on a rainbow and supported by angels, his right hand raised in blessing, crowns the church's entrance door.

It's an amazing sight as you enter the church and repays a closer look when you leave.

Walk around the outside of the church and you'll notice the pockmarked walls, injuries sustained during the English Civil War. The town is said to have changed hands seven times during that tumultuous period and the Abbey was at the heart of it.

Churchyards often reveal some strange tales but surely few can match the poetic gravestone of young Hannah Twynnoy. A local barmaid who died in the jaws of a tiger in 1703, she was said to be the first person to be killed by a tiger in England.

METROPOLITAN CATHEDRAL OF CHRIST THE KING, LIVERPOOL

England's most striking Catholic cathedral was consecrated on Whit Sunday, 1967. At the time Liverpool was still scarred by wartime bombing and suddenly this innovative white building was rising triumphantly, all newness and light.

Liverpudlians affectionately dubbed its distinctive shape 'Paddy's Wigwam' and 'the Mersey Funnel'. Clad in Portland stone, 50 years on it still looks almost new.

The decision to build a cathedral for the newly created Catholic Diocese of Liverpool came in the early 1850s, when the city's Catholic population was increasing dramatically as a result of the devastating Irish potato famine. Edward Welby Pugin's bold High Gothic design with a 300-foot (91-metre) spire would be built on the grounds of the seminary at St Edward's College, set on a ridge in the Everton district with a commanding view over the River Mersey.

After three years, with only the Lady Chapel completed, funds were required elsewhere. Further construction was halted and for over a century the chapel served as the Parish Church of Our Lady Immaculate.

The wish for a cathedral did not go away, however, and the project was revived when Archbishop Downey purchased the former Brownlow Hill Workhouse site at the top of Hope Street in 1930. Sir Edwin Lutyens was appointed as architect.

Lutyens envisioned a vast, classical cathedral that would not only outdo the great neo-Gothic Anglican cathedral being built further down the road, but its dome was to be even larger than that of St Peter's in Rome. Construction began in 1933 and continued into the early years of the Second World War but ceased in 1941, recommencing in 1956. The crypt was structurally finished when the project was cancelled. Escalating costs had made the grandiose scheme far too expensive.

A scaled down version was mooted but rejected and in 1960, Archbishop (later Cardinal) Heenan launched a worldwide competition to find an architect who could design a cathedral for the changing liturgical times. The entire congregation should be able to see the altar in order to participate more fully in the Mass. The structure must stand above the huge Lutyens crypt, the cost should be reasonable and the building erected quickly.

Of the 300 entries received, Sir Frederick Gibberd's plan for a Modernist church-in-the-round that could seat 2,300 people, with an unobstructed view for all, was accepted. Construction began in 1962 and lasted just five years.

Shaped like an inverted funnel, with concrete boomerang-like buttresses, a central cone and stained-glass lantern tower crowned by thorn-like pinnacles, it could hardly look more different from the other 20th-century cathedral on the appropriately named Hope Street.

Set on a plateau above the city, the approach is via a wide flight of 56 banner-lined steps and across the open piazza that forms a roof over Lutyens' crypt. Four bells hang high on a soaring concrete facade, decorated with a carved relief symbolising the three crosses on Calvary. The main doors resemble bronze but were made from fibreglass.

Bathed in vivid light from John Piper's lantern tower, the interior is dramatic. At its heart, raised on a sanctuary platform surrounded by semicircles of seating, is the high altar. It took local stonemason Leslie Rumsey two years of searching before he found this ten-foot- (three-metre-) long, nineteen-ton block of white marble near Skopje in Macedonia. Elizabeth Frink's slim bronze crucifix hovers above the altar while high overhead, suspended from the roof, there's a huge crowning baldachin formed from aluminium rods.

Gibberd interpreted perfectly Archbishop Heenan's demand that 'the attention of all who enter should be arrested and held by the altar'.

There is much else for the eye to alight on and appreciate, not least the spectacular embroidered hangings lining the

Photo: Tony Hisgett

walls, designed and created in the Cathedral Art Studio. Then there are the nine encircling side chapels. Defined by blue stained glass, each one is a repository of fine contemporary ecclesiastical art.

Outside the Blessed Sacrament Chapel, look for the glass rotunda where an elegant spiral staircase leads down to Lutyens' crypt, so vast that the cathedral above barely covers a quarter of its surface area. Here are two great halls and smaller chapels amid fine deep purple brickwork, towering grey granite columns, vaulted passageways and high barrel ceilings. It's an insight into what might have been.

The Pontifical Hall, which initially served as the cathedral while building work was taking place overhead, contains exhibitions and the cathedral's gleaming Treasury. Its most striking feature is the huge rolling stone gate, a six-ton fretted marble disc opening to the Chapel of Relics. Lined with travertine marble, the chapel houses the tombs of three former Archbishops of Liverpool.

Lutyens planned the 130-foot- (40-metre-) long Crypt Hall as a sacristy where 100 priests could robe. Today it is used for dinners, conferences, exhibitions, and the Liverpool Beer Festival.

Daily services take place in the chapel dedicated to St Nicholas, the city's patron saint, which has beautiful wall hangings and evocative sculptures. Mirroring it in size, a former chapel now hosts chamber concerts.

Lutyens created a twelve-foot- (3.6-metre-) high architectural model of his planned masterpiece. You can see it, beautifully restored, at the Museum of Liverpool.

Archbishop Heenan wanted a cathedral for our time, a modern cathedral for a modern city. Gibberd's design has had it detractors, but today is much loved by both the people of the city and its many thousands of visitors.

NORWICH CATHEDRAL

Norwich Cathedral, dedicated to the Holy and Undivided Trinity, is the most complete Romanesque cathedral in England. It is also one of the loveliest of all the cathedrals in Britain. Other than having a new spire added in the 15th century, when the nave was given a stone vault and a clerestory, it remains pretty faithful to its 12th-century plan.

In a characteristic assertion of their power and authority, the conquering Normans first built a castle and then, having moved the bishop's see from Thetford to Norwich, a cathedral.

Begun in 1096, its first bishop, the ambitious and entrepreneurial Herbert de Losinga, demolished about a third of the thriving town for his project. Homes and churches were swept away and the site was levelled. It would have a nave longer than that at Canterbury and the highest tower of its time. Tall defensive walls would surround the whole precinct: the cathedral, the Benedictine monastery buildings and his palace.

Today two fine medieval gates mark the entrance to the cathedral's picturesque walled close. The tower, with its distinctive porthole-like tracery is still the highest Norman tower in the land, while the remarkable two-storey monastic cloisters are the largest in England. Only Salisbury Cathedral (page 197) has a spire taller than that at Norwich. Built from smooth, creamy Caen limestone, it is a spectacular building.

The interior is equally stunning. In the long nave, fourteen bays of rounded Romanesque arches rise up to Gothic clerestory windows and the Perpendicular flare of the vault. Muscular meets soaring lightness and the two styles flow together seamlessly.

A gallery of over 400 elaborately carved and coloured bosses adorn the centre line of the vault. They tell stories and events from the Old and New Testaments in chronological order. While the wheeled mirror helps, they are so high up that you really need binoculars to see them better. With each keystone capturing a whole scene in remarkable detail, they are triumphs of medieval art. The cathedral contains the greatest collection of roof bosses in the world, over 1,000 of them in all.

Enormous drum-like piers grooved with spirals break the earlier symmetry of the nave. Bishop Herbert had them built there to frame the nave altar of the Holy Cross, their design echoing that of the shrine of St Peter in Rome.

In another reference to the early Church, he placed the bishop's throne on a platform above the high altar in the east end. Its siting follows the tradition of early Christian worship in Roman basilicas and, uniquely in British cathedrals, Norwich has retained the throne in this position throughout its history.

The modern chair incorporates pre-Conquest stones and a flue hidden beneath it leads out to a niche down in the ambulatory behind the platform. The niche may once have held relics or treasures and now displays an icon of the Resurrection.

Bishop Herbert's tomb is set in the floor before the high altar, overlooked by the ornate and colourfully painted chantry chapel of Bishop James Goldwell. He died in 1499, having completed the cathedral's spire and inserted the fine stone vaulting in the nave. The chapel was badly damaged by iconoclasts and a Cromwellian musket ball remains lodged in one side.

On the pulpitum screen supporting the grand organ, don't miss the rare painting in memory of a 17th-century cathedral organist, in which two singing men holding music partbooks and wreaths mourn his passing.

In the quire, the oak stalls with their intricately-carved canopies date mainly from the 15th century, as are the misericords, about 60 of them, their images a mix of animals, birds, scripture and (often humorous) depictions of medieval life. A new addition shows a goalkeeper in action, a tribute to Norwich Football Club.

Surmounted by later clerestory windows with delicate tracery and a boss-studded vault, England's finest Norman apse is still surrounded by original chapels and chantries. The cathedral's greatest treasure is in St Luke's Chapel. Known as the Despenser Retable, painted in Norwich and dating from the late 14th century, its five panels vividly depict scenes from Christ's Passion, death and Resurrection.

St Saviour's Chapel is where you might expect to find a Lady Chapel. It stands on the site of a Saxon church, demolished for Bishop Herbert's new cathedral, and is now a memorial to those who died in the First World War. A door leads out to the grave of Edith Cavell, the pioneering Norfolk-born nurse who sheltered Allied soldiers in occupied Belgium and was executed by a German firing squad in 1915.

The cathedral's medieval glass was destroyed during the Reformation and the English Civil War, but in 1963 enough medieval pieces were gleaned from a variety of Norwich sources, including the bishop's palace, to create the Erpingham Window in the presbytery's north aisle.

Otherwise the windows are mainly Victorian, introduced during a major refurbishment in 1830, with contemporary glass in the north transept and nearby aisle. Fragments of medieval wall paintings survive, the best collection being in the Treasury, set above an arch off the north transept.

The oldest of the story-telling bosses, 394 in all and the

Photo: Jorge Pena Ramos

easiest to see, are in the vaulted roof of the impressive cloisters. Many show visions from the Book of Revelation and were inserted during rebuilding in the 14th century.

The townspeople had plenty of reasons to revolt against the priory and in 1272 a riot ensued, lasting for three days. Fire destroyed the original Norman cloister, most of the monastic buildings and even reached the cathedral itself. After King Edward I intervened, the dispute was settled and work began on rebuilding the cloister in 1297. It was not completed until 1430, construction having been stalled by the Black Death that killed a quarter of the city's population. As the stone tracery in the open windows reveals, by the time building resumed the Decorated style had been overtaken by the newly fashionable Perpendicular.

Surrounding a grassy quadrangle on all sides, the long covered cloister walkways that connected the cathedral with various monastic buildings contain some of the finest stone carving in England. In the north corner leading to the nave, look for the decorative carving above the Prior's doorway and notice the ledges beneath the arches of 'cupboards', worn smooth by the feet of monks collecting their books for services.

On the south side an entrance now leads to the striking new Refectory restaurant, built on the site of the monastic refectory. In the west, the doorway that led to the priory's guest hall now opens into the Hostry Visitor and Education Centre. Both are fine examples of innovative modern architecture and well worth visiting.

As you leave, do wander through the handsome close, which has over 80 listed buildings within its 44 acres (17.8 hectares). Visit the herb and Japanese gardens and meander down to the watergate at Pulls Ferry on the River Wensum, where barges once landed the building stone from quarries in Caen in Normandy. From there, the Riverside Walk promises a peacefully scenic stroll.

PETERBOROUGH CATHEDRAL

Peterborough Cathedral's west front – a vast, Gothic triple-arched portico as wide as it is tall – is unique in Christendom and the 13th-century painted nave ceiling is unique in size and age in all Europe. Katharine of Aragon is buried here; Mary, Queen of Scots was interred at Peterborough after her beheading at nearby Fotheringhay Castle. At the heart of the busy, ever-expanding city, the Cathedral Church of St Peter, St Paul and St Andrew and its precincts are an island of serenity in a sea of shops.

When the first church was founded here in 655 in the reign of the Anglo-Saxon King Paeda, it was a monastic settlement on the edge of the remote and waterlogged fens. A largely uninhabited area, it was well stocked with fish, wildfowl and reeds for thatching. There was a fine quarry a few miles away at Barnack and timber could be had from Rockingham Forest, with the River Nene handy for transport.

Viking raiders destroyed the settlement in 870, the monks were killed and Christianity all but wiped out in the region as the Danish settlers had their own gods. Around a century later, Ethelwold, Bishop of Winchester, founded an abbey and monastery on the site under the Rule of St Benedict. Dedicated to St Peter, it thrived until an accidental fire swept through it in 1116.

Work began in 1118 on the Abbey Church that would become Peterborough Cathedral and, additions and renovations aside, the structure of the building has remained essentially as it was when it was consecrated in 1238.

Given the dramatic west front, the visitor could be forgiven for thinking that the rest might be a bit of a let-down. But no, it more than lives up to its promise, for this is one of the finest Romanesque church interiors in the world.

Blessedly clear of clutter, the vista down the long, light and airy nave is of an arcade of wide curving arches and sturdy shafted piers, cool and solidly grounded in creamy Barnack stone. They rise in three storeys to the glorious wooden ceiling, hand painted between 1230 and 1250 and composed of lozenge panels, each one containing a different image. In darkly medieval colours, although the ceiling has been painted over twice, the design and pattern are original. Wheel one of the mirrored trolleys along to see the detail more clearly.

Made and erected in the 1970s, a huge wooden cross with the powerful figure of Christ in gold on a bright red background, is a striking focal point above the central altar at the end of the nave. In contrast, the bowl of the font at the cathedral's entrance, carved from local Alwalton marble, is from the 13th century. It was rescued from a nearby garden in the 1820s where it had been used as a flower tub. Look for the fish tucked in among the lilies and leaves.

High up on the wall behind you, Old Scarlett, a celebrated local character, is commemorated in a portrait, rhyme and faded fresco. The local gravedigger, he died in 1594 at the age of 98, his claim to fame being that he buried two queens in the cathedral. Legend suggests that he was the inspiration for the gravedigger in Shakespeare's *Hamlet*. Watching over all who enter and leave the building, he is portrayed in 'strength and sturdye limm', his spade in one hand, his keys in the other, and a skull at his feet.

A fine golden eagle lectern from the late 15th century stands boldly at the entrance to the quire with its beautifully hand-carved oak quire stalls full of exquisite lace-like detail. The lectern survived the ravages of the English Civil War when the cathedral and the town (with its Royalist sympathies) suffered badly under Cromwell's brutish troops in 1643.

The story goes that the iconoclasts, told that the weighty lectern wasn't made of gold, snipped off a bit of its feathered wing to make sure. Satisfied that it wasn't such rich pickings after all, and being heavy to cart off, they left it behind, exhausted perhaps by the two days it had taken to demolish the elaborate stone pulpitum (screen) and its organ. By the time the Parliamentarians had finished their work, nearly all the cathedral's stained glass had been destroyed, the library's fine collection of books and manuscripts burned and the cloisters and Lady Chapel demolished.

The crossing is pure Norman, its north and south transepts unaltered except in their window glass – don't miss the brightly coloured 19th-century windows by Dante Gabriel Rosetti in the south transept.

In this transept are three small chapels, the most decorated being that dedicated to St Oswald, which even has a watching tower from which monks could safeguard what had been Peterborough's most cherished relic – the arm of St Oswald (stolen, 'tis said, in the year 1000 from Bamburgh Castle by an abbey monk in an attempt to gain favour with his abbot). It disappeared during the Reformation.

The central tower has been rebuilt twice, most recently in the 19th century when pieces of falling masonry made the cathedral unsafe. The beams and the roof bosses of the very fine 14th-century wooden ceiling were replaced and it's a neck-cricking but joyous view from below.

Photo: Bischling

The great Romanesque arcade of arches continues into the sanctuary where the high altar has an impressive – if somewhat incongruous – intricately carved, pink marble ciborium (altar canopy). It was added in the 1880s when the whole central and eastern end of the building required refurbishment after the rebuilding of the central tower.

The sanctuary has a fine marble tesserae pavement and overhead a stunning early-16th-century vaulted ceiling panelled in navy blue and gold. The sky blue and gold ceiling painting of Christ in Majesty was restored at the same time, have suffered from Parliamentarian musket shot.

Alongside the sanctuary, two Tudor queens are remembered. In the north aisle, Katharine of Aragon, discarded first wife of King Henry VIII, is given the dignity of her title Queen of England above the simple marble slab that indicates her grave. Peterborough was the nearest abbey to Kimbolton Castle, where she died in January 1536, and every year a service is held here in her memory.

The body of another sad queen, Mary, Queen of Scots, was brought to Peterborough five months after her execution at Fotheringhay Castle in 1587. In 1612 her remains were exhumed and taken to Westminster Abbey for reburial on the orders of her son, King James I of England. Her memorial is in the south aisle.

Ahead, the magnificent 'New Building' is a whirl of fabulous fan vaulting by the leading Tudor architect John Wastell, a design he went on to develop further for the ceiling of King's College Chapel, Cambridge (page 112). Built in the early 1500s as a processional route around the east end of the building, it contains some interesting stained-glass windows and the Hedda Stone. A grave marker for Abbot Hedda and his monks, murdered by the Danes when they sacked the original abbey, the Hedda Stone is believed to date from 870.

Peterborough Abbey was dissolved in 1539 during the Reformation and its land and properties confiscated. Instead of tearing down the church, however, King Henry VIII created a new bishop (the former abbot) in 1541 and the great Abbey was transformed into Peterborough Cathedral.

ROCHESTER CATHEDRAL

Rochester Cathedral's story goes back to Pope Gregory I's first missionaries to Saxon England: Augustine (in 597) and Justus (in 601). Soon after he had founded the Canterbury diocese, in 604 Augustine consecrated Justus as Bishop of Rochester to found England's second cathedral. It was dedicated to St Andrew and built on land given by King Ethelbert of Kent.

The town's strategic position, on the old Roman crossing point on the River Medway, made it an important stopping place on the route between London and Canterbury and onwards across the English Channel. It also made it vulnerable to attack. Mercians, Wessex men and Danes all raided Rochester in the following centuries. The conquering Normans took over much of the town to build their huge castle. One of the earliest to be built in stone, it had (and still has) the tallest Norman keep in England.

The new Norman bishop in 1077 was Gandulf, a monk and noted architect who counted among his legacies the massive keep of the Tower of London. He established a community of Benedictine monks at Rochester in 1083 and began work on a new cathedral, situated strikingly close to the castle, which he also had a hand in building. It was consecrated in 1130, at a ceremony attended by King Henry I.

Today the west facade is a fine example of Norman architecture. It's the only surviving cathedral front from this period in England. The main doorway with its elaborate stone carving is splendid. Its five semi-circular arches encompass a tympanum in which Christ sits enthroned in majesty attended by angels and the winged symbols of the Four Evangelists: Matthew, Mark, Luke and John. The (heavily eroded) figures on either side of the doorway are of King Solomon and the Queen of Sheba.

With its powerful piers and rounded chevron-patterned arches, the nave is unmistakably Norman. Gandulf's original nave was destroyed by fire in 1137, but rebuilt in the Romanesque style. Two bays at the eastern end have the taller, pointed arches of the Early English Gothic style of the 1200s – an indication that at one time the plan had been for the whole nave to be remodelled.

Added in the mid-1400s, the great west window is in the Perpendicular Gothic style, which when seen from the outside breaks up the cohesion of the west front's Norman architecture. Its Victorian glass, depicting Old Testament figures and Christian saints with military connections, was inserted in memory of the Royal Engineers.

Rochester's nave has had a battered history. As well as enduring several major fires it was used as a base for quartering troops and their horses during various sieges of the nearby castle, and as a carpenters' workshop and alehouse during the Commonwealth period in the 1650s.

Its sturdy arcades end at the crossing, where a wide flight of steps leads up to the creamy stone pulpitum. This screen, which separates the nave (used by the townspeople) from the quire (where the monks worshipped), was installed during major restoration work by the Victorian architect Sir George Gilbert Scott.

The four statues on each side of its central arch represent saints and kings of special significance to the cathedral. These include King Ethelbert, who gave the land for the first cathedral; St Andrew, to whom it was dedicated; and St Justus, the first Bishop of Rochester.

Also commemorated is Bishop John Fisher, one of two Rochester bishops martyred during the Reformation. Fisher, having been tutor to the young Prince Henry, was a strong supporter of King Henry VIII until it came to the matter of his divorce from Katharine of Aragon, when he sided with Rome. He was beheaded in 1535 and canonised four centuries later.

The pulpitum supports the magnificent organ, its casing and pipes colourfully painted and decorated in the Gothic Revival style of George Gilbert Scott.

The north transept's doorway was the medieval pilgrims' entrance to the cathedral. After the murder of Thomas Becket in 1170, Rochester found itself on the pilgrim route to Canterbury. By 1201, however, it had its own saint, William of Perth.

William, a Scottish baker, was on pilgrimage to the Holy Land when, on leaving Rochester, he was murdered by his servant just outside the town. The woman who found him claimed to have been cured of madness and his body was taken to be buried in the cathedral. More miracles followed and pilgrim donations at his shrine were sufficient to fund the building of a new east end.

The vibrant fresco that now fills a wall in this north transept entrance was painted by the celebrated Russian iconographer, Sergei Fyodorov, and dedicated in 2004 on the 1,400th anniversary of the cathedral's founding. In the

Photo: Poliphilo

Byzantine style of the Eastern Orthodox Church, it depicts Jesus' baptism in the River Jordan, St Augustine's baptism of King Ethelbert and the conversion and baptism of countless Saxon people in the River Medway.

The stone steps up to the quire and sanctuary have been so worn down by the feet of pilgrims across the centuries that for safety's sake a modern wooden staircase has been installed to cover them.

Until the Reformation, Rochester had the shrines of three saints: Paulinus, one of the early missionaries from Rome, Bishop of Rochester and the first Bishop of York; Ithamar, England's first Saxon-born bishop; and the commoner, William of Perth. Rochester's monastic community was one of the last to be dissolved and in 1540 the cathedral of St Andrew was refounded in the name of Christ and the Blessed Virgin Mary.

That was also the year when, on New Year's Day, King Henry VIII met Anne of Cleves for the first time at Rochester Priory. It was not a happy occasion: the king declared himself 'greatly disappointed'. The marriage did not last.

After the stone simplicity of the Norman nave, entering the heavily restored east end of the cathedral is like stepping into another world. Here all is Early English Gothic and the walls of the large quire are painted a rich red, patterned with emblems of King Edward III. The stalls are Victorian but contain remnants of those put in around 1227.

The north wall of the quire has a fragment of a 13th-century wall painting depicting a Wheel of Fortune. The figure at the centre, Fortuna, controls the ups and downs of men clambering up the wheel in pursuit of earthly money, power and status.

The sanctuary is spacious, the high altar placed against the eastern wall of lancet windows set into Gothic arches. On its north side is the effigy-topped tomb of John de Sheppey, 14th-century Treasurer of England and Bishop of Rochester, which still retains its original colouring.

In the south quire aisle there's a brass plaque memorial to Charles Dickens. The author had warm childhood memories of Rochester and in later life lived at nearby Gad's Hill. The city appears as a location in his first book, *The Pickwick Papers*, and is the central setting in his last, the unfinished *The Mystery of Edwin Drood*.

He had expressed the wish to be buried in the graveyard at Rochester Cathedral, but a grateful nation decided otherwise and he was interred in Poet's Corner at Westminster Abbey. A memorial service is held for him in the cathedral every year.

Then you come to Hamo de Hythe's doorway. A monk who became a bishop, Hamo de Hythe contributed to the building of the cathedral but his greatest legacy is this exquisitely carved stone doorway dating from 1343. Once the monks' night-time entrance and now leading to the library, it has dozens of faces and figures depicting the beliefs and teachings of the Church in the Middle Ages.

Follow the steps down into the beautifully restored crypt. Part dates back to Bishop Gandulf's time but it was mainly built in the 12th century and extends under the east end of the cathedral. Dickens described the aisles between the twenty freestanding columns as 'lanes of light'. The simply furnished St Ithamar's Chapel is a wonderful space in which to ponder and pray.

The crypt also hosts an interactive exhibition, Bridge Works. Essentially about the bridges that have crossed the Medway at Rochester since Roman times, it leans heavily on the *Textus Roffensis*, Rochester's Mystery Book. Containing the earliest surviving code of English law, it was written in

Old English (Anglo-Saxon) and Latin in a script unique to documents produced at Rochester Priory and known as Rochester Prickly. Pre-dating the Magna Carta, it is one of the most important books to survive in England, yet few people know of its existence.

ROMSEY ABBEY

Dedicated to St Mary and St Ethelflaeda, Romsey Abbey was founded in 907 as a Saxon nunnery by Edward the Elder, son of Alfred the Great. Sixty years later it was refounded under the Rule of St Benedict by his grandson, Edgar the Peaceful, and continued as a Benedictine convent until the dissolution of the monasteries in 1539.

The fact that local townspeople worshipped in part of its church at that time probably saved Romsey Abbey from demolition and the town was allowed to buy the building for £100. It remains the largest parish church in Hampshire.

The spacious nave, with its three tiers of creamy limestone columns soaring to a high barrel roof, gives an unobstructed view to the simply dressed high altar. Building began on this grand Norman church in 1120 and took over a hundred years to complete. During this time fashions in architecture changed and the last three bays at the west end of the nave, built around 1240, display the pointed arches of the Early English Gothic style.

There is much fine Romanesque stone carving to admire throughout the church, particularly on the numerous arches at every level. At the east end, don't forget to look up, for the decorative carvings on the capitals tell many a tale.

A colourful curtain greets you as you turn right by the carved wood lectern at the top of the nave. Designed and made by students of Southampton College of Arts in 1961, it depicts saints with their symbols and covers a doorway that was once where nuns entered the church from their convent buildings.

The south transept is given over to the Chapel of St Nicholas, where families who lived at the nearby historic Broadlands estate, much loved by members of the royal family, are remembered. Its most famous 20th-century resident, Lord Louis Mountbatten, is buried in the chapel under the simple engraved statement 'Admiral of the Fleet, Earl Mountbatten of Burma, 1900–1979. In Honour Bound.'

On the wall is a standout memorial to John and Grissell St Barbe, whose family acquired the estate after the Dissolution. They were buried on the same day in 1658, having died of 'sweating sickness'. Below the couple and an interesting verse are the charmingly portrayed figures of their four sons. Three are holding a sprig of leaves, indicating that they were alive when their parents died. The fourth child, empty handed, pre-deceased them.

Don't miss the modern sculpture of St Nicholas, bishop and patron saint of sailors, by the English sculptor Peter Eugene Ball. It was designed around a piece of driftwood found on a beach near Southampton.

Ahead, in the apse at the east end of the south quire aisle, is St Anne's Chapel. It contains the Abbey's greatest treasure, a Saxon rood (crucifix) that dates from the 960s. It shows Christ on the cross with Roman soldiers below and St Mary and St John at his side, with two cherubim on high waiting to escort him to Heaven. It's thought that the nuns may have received it from King Edgar when he refounded the nunnery.

En route there, stop to look at the glass case containing the Threadgold Treasury. Its highlights are the Deed of Sale, signed by King Henry VIII, that transferred the abbey church to the town, and a lovely illuminated psalter from the 15th century which has St Ethelflaeda's festivals marked in red letters.

There are four chapels at the east end of the church, the two in the centre being dedicated to the Abbey's patron saints, St Mary the mother of Jesus and the 10th-century abbess St Ethelflaeda.

St Mary's Chapel, where the tomb of a former abbess forms the altar, has the pale remains of an early 13th-century wall painting. The tomb of an unidentified 13th-century abbess in St Ethelflaeda's Chapel has the rather unnerving image of her hand reaching out from under its lid to grasp onto her crozier.

The fourth chapel, set into an apse, is dedicated to St George. Over the altar, 'Christus Rex' is another striking sculpture by Peter Eugene Ball and on the floor are 700-year-old tiles, some depicting knights in armour and crusader knights on horseback.

Nearby in the north quire aisle, guarded by a heavy curtain, is a rare and delicate piece of medieval fabric from the nunnery. Known as the Romsey Cope, it was made in the late 15th century from green Italian velvet and embroidered with stars in silver gilt thread.

In the quire itself, bronze silhouettes of Lord Mountbatten and his wife Edwina define the Broadlands Pew, still in use by members of his family.

As you pass under the crossing, don't miss the gorgeously painted Jacobean ceiling that forms the floor of the ringing chamber above. At ground level, a glass covering reveals foundations of the 10th-century Saxon church that this abbey replaced.

Before the Dissolution, the north aisle and transept were used by local townspeople as their Parish Church of St Lawrence, suitably screened off from the rest of the Abbey and the nuns. Today the north transept holds the Chapel of St Lawrence.

The wooden Italianate reredos behind the altar dates from around 1525. Its top depicts a row of saints set above a panel with Christ rising from the tomb surrounded by astonished Roman soldiers. The nun looking on may be the last abbess of Romsey Abbey, Elizabeth Ryprose.

Leave the Abbey through the south door and turn left to see the 11th-century Saxon rood depicting Christ reigning triumphant from the cross, with the Hand of God reaching down to him from above. Next to it is the splendidly decorated Abbess's Doorway, formerly the entrance into the church from the Abbey cloisters.

The exterior of the building is adorned with 400 carved stone corbels and gargoyles, their subjects including people, cats, demons, animals and fantasy beasts, even an ancient fertility figure. It's well worth a search for them.

ST ALBANS CATHEDRAL

Standing on the place where Alban, England's first saint and martyr, was buried over 1,700 years ago, the Cathedral and Abbey Church of St Alban is the oldest site of continuous Christian worship in Britain. It's an extraordinary building, boldly displaying its chequered history in a mix of architectural styles that may surprise, fascinate, delight and at times dismay.

It owes its existence to Alban, a Briton who in the 3rd century converted to Christianity when he sheltered a fugitive priest. For this he was beheaded by the Romans in Verulamium, their city in the valley below today's St Albans. There are many legends associated with his martyrdom, and the priest he protected was only named as Amphibalus in a much later historical document, but there's evidence that a cult grew up around him. In 795, King Offa of Mercia founded a Benedictine abbey over his tomb.

In 1077 its first Norman abbot, Paul of Caen, set about rebuilding the church, turning to the ruined site of Verulamium for materials, recycling Roman brick, tiles and flint for its construction. The cathedral's tower, 144 feet (44.5 metres) high and weighing 5,000 tons, is the only Norman great crossing tower still standing in England.

With the shrine of Britain's first martyr, the importance of the monastery grew. Counted among its monks were theologians, philosophers and artists, poets and scientists. The scriptorium was famed for the quality of its books and among its famous chroniclers was Matthew Paris, who produced an illustrated life of St Alban in the 13th century. Nicholas Breakespeare, who in 1154, as Adrian IV, was the first (and only) English pope, was born in the area. His father Robert was an official of the abbey and was buried in the chapter house.

Until the Reformation, the Benedictine abbey was the premier monastery in England. It was huge and being only a day's ride from London popular with kings, courtiers and their attendant retinues. King Henry III is said to have made nine visits. The stables could house 200 horses and by the 15th century the abbey's guest hall had its own team of huntsmen and falconers to entertain the stream of important visitors.

The outside of the church was rendered with lime plaster,

partly to protect it from the elements, partly to hide the building materials. With the plaster long gone, today ferns sprout between the flint, rubble and red Roman brick, all part of the cathedral's distinctive character.

At the Reformation the monastery buildings were demolished but the grand gateway, erected in the 1390s, survived and today forms part of St Albans School. The local townspeople bought the abbey for use as their parish church – a designation it retained when it was elevated to cathedral status in 1887.

However, the cost of upkeep proved too high and by the 19th century it was in very bad shape. In 1856, the distinguished Gothic Revivalist architect Sir George Gilbert Scott was called in to rescue it and the best restoration work was carried out during his years as cathedral architect. When he died in 1878 Sir Edmund Beckett, later Lord Grimthorpe, a wealthy retired barrister, offered to fund the cost of the work – to his own design.

Grimthorpe was an amateur architect and some of the changes he made were disastrous. He rebuilt the west front, totally out of character with the rest of the building, and even had himself portrayed in the porch as St Matthew, sprouting wings. His work was the stimulus for the founding of the Society for the Protection of Ancient Buildings, to prevent anything like that happening again. However, thanks to Victorian restorers, the abbey was saved.

The long nave of the cathedral – at 276 feet (85 metres) one of the longest in the country – displays a contrasting mix of architectural styles.

At the top on the north side, Abbot Paul's plain rounded Romanesque arches are painted in alternating blocks of ochre and cream – being built from Roman bricks and rubble then plastered over, they couldn't be carved.

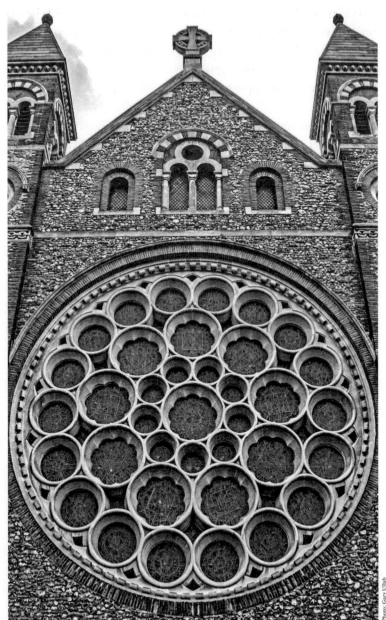

Photo: Gary Ullah

It's in this section that we find the outstanding medieval wall paintings that are among the cathedral's great treasures. Whitewashed over after the dissolution of the monastery in 1539, they were rediscovered in 1862. Although damaged during the cleaning process, they are still in remarkable condition.

When the nave was extended westwards in the late 12th and early 13th centuries it was built from soft limestone in the new Early English Gothic style, with pointed arches. Then in 1323 two of the Norman pillars at the top of the nave on the south side crashed down. Rebuilding was done in Decorated Gothic.

The stone rood screen separating the nave from the monastic part of the church was installed in the mid-14th century, when it was richly ornamented with carvings and statues. They all went at the Reformation and the niches remained empty for nearly 500 years. They were filled in 2015 with the colourful, and unnervingly lifelike, figures of Christian martyrs, from Saints Alban and Amphibalus to the 20th-century's Dietrich Bonhoeffer and Archbishop (now Saint) Oscar Romero, by contemporary sculptor Rory Young.

The quire, the main monastic area in the past, was rebuilt during the Victorian restoration by the architect John Oldrid Scott. It was his father, Sir George Gilbert Scott, who had the splendid flooring of the crossing made by Minton Hollins & Co. in a pattern based on the few tiles that survived from the medieval abbey. Watching over the world-renowned organ that towers behind the carved wood quire stalls, the wonderful panelled wood ceiling, probably painted in the 14th century, was discovered during the restoration.

You are now into the crossing, the first part of the abbey church to be built. For nigh on a thousand years, the four massive piers have supported the crossing tower. Like their

Norman sisters in the nave, their great arches are painted in a chequerboard of ochre and cream.

Look up to the tower ceiling, refurbished in 1951. A copy of the 15th-century original (which remains in place above it), its panels display heraldry and the red and white roses associated with the Houses of Lancaster and York. Two battles in the Wars of the Roses were fought in St Albans, in 1455 (won by the Yorkists) and 1461 (won by the Lancastrians).

Ahead are the magnificent high altar screen and chantry chapels under a lovely 13th-century wooden ceiling. Made from oak donated by King Henry II, it was painted during the 15th century.

The medieval altar screen is filled with Victorian statues representing Christ, saints and characters from the history of British Christianity. The reredos, carved to a design by Sir Alfred Gilbert, famed as the creator of 'Eros' in London's Piccadilly Circus, is made of marble, glass and iridescent paua (abalone) shells from New Zealand.

The two transepts are wide and spacious. At the triforium level of the south transept, Saxon pillars and exposed Roman brick are an example of Norman recycling. The north transept is lit by a vast rose window, controversially inserted by Lord Grimthorpe. His design was of clear glass; its vivid colour came in 1989. Designed by the renowned stained-glass artist Alan Younger, it contains over 8,000 pieces of glass and was unveiled by Diana, Princess of Wales.

As you leave the north transept, don't miss the unusual 14th-century wall painting depicting Doubting Thomas, which pilgrims would have passed on their way to the shrine of St Alban.

His shrine chapel is indeed a very special place. A red silk canopy embroidered with gold thread hangs above the ornately carved Purbeck Marble shrine pedestal dating from the early 14th century. Smashed into smithereens at the dissolution of the monastery, it was reconstructed in 1872 from over 2,000 small pieces found when blocked up arches were being dismantled. The shrine was rededicated after further restoration took place in 1993.

Guarding it is a rare watching loft. Carved from solid oak in around 1400, the oldest such loft still surviving in England, from here monks and townspeople kept a close eye on the pilgrims and the treasures and gifts they brought to the shrine. The frieze is carved with fascinating scenes from daily life, best seen from the back of the loft in the north quire aisle, where the shrine of St Amphibalus awaits restoration.

Finally you arrive at the lovely 14th-century Lady Chapel. When the townspeople took over the abbey church in 1553, they walled off the chapel and for 300 years it was used as a grammar school. A public passageway ran between it and the church. When the school was transferred to the medieval gateway in 1891, the Lady Chapel once again became part of the church and was sympathetically restored.

Demolishing the dividing wall uncovered another treasure: a very fine wall painting of St William of York, dating from around 1308. Tucked away in a corner of St Alban's shrine chapel, by the watching loft, much of its rich colouring has survived and it's a gem.

Quirky and full of character, St Albans Cathedral is much used and much loved. A centre of ecumenical worship, it is the only cathedral to hold regular services for members of other denominations, including monthly Free Church, German Lutheran and Russian Orthodox services and a weekly Roman Catholic Mass. Its story is not as widely known as perhaps it should be, but with the completion of the innovative, £7 million 'Alban, Britain's First Saint' development project, that could change.

ST DAVIDS CATHEDRAL, PEMBROKESHIRE

Most British cathedrals are in the centre of a city or, like those in Durham (page 63) and Lincoln (page 121), stand high above the townscape at their feet. St Davids, however, snuggles into a valley. The approach from town through the 14th-century Tower Gate is much higher than the cathedral so, rather unexpectedly, your first sight of the dusky pink sandstone building is a bird's-eye view of its roofs.

In the 6th century, St David (Dewi Sant), Wales' patron saint, founded a monastery and church here, hidden away among dense bushes and trees in a boggy valley by the River Alun. Stories of the monks' ascetic lives of prayer, study and hard labour in the fields attracted pilgrims but their location near the Pembrokeshire coast, on the sea route to Ireland, also attracted the unwanted attention of passing Vikings, raiders and pirates.

The monastery became a renowned religious and intellectual centre, but down the centuries raiders murdered at least two of its bishops and by 1089 St David's shrine had been vandalised and stripped of the precious metals that adorned it.

William the Conqueror came here to pray in 1081, though he may have been more interested in its strategic peninsula position and proximity to Ireland. The Normans saw the Celtic religion as inferior to their own and the Welsh Church as a threat to their controlling rule, therefore in need of reform.

In 1115, King Henry I appointed Bernard as the first Norman bishop of St Davids. He began building a new cathedral, dedicated in 1131, and shrewdly persuaded the Pope to make St Davids a place of pilgrimage: two journeys

Photo: W. Bulach

169

to St Davids were equivalent to one to Rome. That church was rebuilt in the Transitional Norman style in the 1180s and forms the basis of the cathedral today.

The light that floods the 12th-century nave highlights the warm colours of the stone arcade, its alternate round and octagonal piers supporting wide, decoratively carved, Romanesque arches.

The nave's oak ceiling is one of the cathedral's glories. It dates from the early 16th century and is a wonder of exquisite carving, with arches and pendants belying the fact that it is actually flat, suspended from tie beams. Medieval motifs appear in the lace-like detail, along with Renaissance features of dragon-shaped dolphins.

From the back of the nave you can see how the walls lean outwards and the sloping floor means that here you, quite literally, walk up the aisle.

The delicately carved stone pulpitum that separates the nave from the quire was the work of Bishop Henry Gower, who made substantial changes to the building and its surroundings during his tenure from 1328 to 1347. His tomb is housed within the screen, alongside a statue of St David dressed as a medieval bishop.

It was Bishop Gower who built the huge Bishop's Palace that broods nearby. Its still impressive ruins, richly embellished with stone carvings and arcaded parapets, speak of the wealth and power of the church in the 14th century.

One of the stalls in the magnificent quire bears the royal coat of arms – uniquely, the reigning British sovereign is a member of the cathedral chapter. The misericords hidden under the 16th-century seats suggest a mischievous streak in their carvers. Among the faces and mythical beasts, one depicts seasick pilgrims in a boat, another a man with backache. Look up: the tower lantern ceiling is beautiful.

Of the chapels beyond the quire, Holy Trinity has fine fan vaulting, an altar pieced together from medieval fragments and in the original pilgrims' recess, a casket many believed held the bones of St David and St Justinian.

In 1536 during the Reformation, the strongly Protestant Bishop William Barker ripped out St David's shrine, stripping it of its jewels and relics. The tomb of Edmund Tudor, King Henry VII's father, was moved here after the dissolution of the monastery at Carmarthen and placed in front of the high altar. A century later, Oliver Cromwell's troops did serious damage to the building, stripping the roofs of lead, wrecking the medieval library, smashing stained-glass windows and tearing up tomb brasses.

Restoration work took place in the 18th century but it was Sir George Gilbert Scott, the prolific English Gothic Revival architect, who made a major contribution to the look and stability of the cathedral towards the end of the 19th century. Further restoration continued on through the 20th century, including the addition of some fine stained glass.

St David's shrine, visited by many thousands of pilgrims until it was destroyed in the Reformation, has been beautifully restored and was rededicated on St David's Day, 1 March, 2012. Painted and gilded icons of St David and fellow saints sit within the shrine's original niches. The oak canopy above it, painted in medieval colours, replicates that of the 13th-century construction.

It breathes history, but St Davids Cathedral is very much a 21st-century church. Its choir is unique in the United Kingdom in that the top line of the full choir is sung by girl choristers aged eight to eighteen. It is also the seat of the first woman bishop to be elected by the Church in Wales.

Visitors speak of a palpable sense of serenity and spirituality in this cathedral within the Pembrokeshire Coast National

Park on the far south-west coast of Wales. The town of St Davids has city status but in reality is hardly bigger than a village. Its narrow streets can get very crowded during the summer months and especially during St Davids Cathedral Festival, a feast of classical and contemporary music concerts held annually at the end of May.

ST EDMUNDSBURY CATHEDRAL

Light and airily spacious, modern yet ancient, the former Parish Church of St James became St Edmundsbury Cathedral in 1914. It can tell a story from the realms of history into the 21st century. HRH The Prince of Wales hailed the lantern tower, completed in 2005, as 'a spiritual beacon for the new Millennium'.

There was a great Benedictine abbey here, founded by King Cnut in 1020 to house the remains of the martyred Edmund, King of the East Angles, killed by invading Danes in 869 and soon regarded as a saint. Its ruins lie nearby in the peaceful, beautifully cared for Abbey Gardens, a highlight in the pleasing market town of Bury St Edmunds. The abbey's gatehouse, rebuilt in the 14th century, is the main entrance to the gardens.

Of the several churches within the abbey precincts, one was built by Abbot Anselm in the 12th century and dedicated to St James. Unable to fulfil his wish to go on pilgrimage to the saint's shrine, Santiago de Compostela in Spain, instead the Abbot built a church for pilgrims to his abbey, which also served people living on the north side of the town that had grown up around it.

At the beginning of the 16th century, a few years before the abbey was dissolved in 1539, plans were being drawn up to extend the building westwards into the street and work began on a new nave.

The master mason was a local man, John Wastell, famed for his work on King's College Chapel in Cambridge (page 112) and as the architect of Canterbury Cathedral's Bell Harry Tower (page 37), which was the inspiration for the design of St Edmundsbury's own Millennium Tower.

As it was in use by local congregations, St James' survived the abbey's demise. Alterations were made in the 18th and 19th centuries and although it was elevated to cathedral status when the Diocese of St Edmundsbury and Ipswich was created in 1914, it was only after the end of the Second World War that work began on enlarging the building under the renowned architect Stephen Dykes Bower. Real changes took place from the 1960s and lasted until the completion of the cathedral in 2011.

The 19th century saw the church in such a state of disrepair that in 1861 it was declared unsafe. The architect called to its rescue, Sir George Gilbert Scott, wanted the new nave roof to be shallow, similar to the one being replaced. He was overruled. Today the rafters of the high-pitched hammer-beam roof are richly patterned and vibrantly painted in red and green, its decorative angels watching over Scott's pews and terracotta-patterned flooring.

Lining the nave, Wastell's arcades of graceful Gothic arches and tall, slim, unadorned piers look almost Modernist. The stained glass in the aisle windows, depicting scenes from the Old Testament on the north side and the New Testament on the south, is by renowned Victorian designers and makers.

Telling the story of Susannah and the Elders from the Apocrypha, the lower section of one window at the west end

Photo: Martin Pettit

contains 15th-century glass probably made in the Rouen area of France. The baptismal font, a towering, boldly painted and gilded confection, dominates this part of the church.

Stephen Dykes Bower's tall, light-filled crossing perfectly complements Wastell's elegant pale stone nave. That the cathedral looks so appealing today is largely due to Dykes Bower, who as well as serving as the Surveyor to the Fabric at Westminster Abbey was the cathedral architect at St Edmundsbury for over 40 years.

A dedicated Gothic Revivalist, to his serene and seamless blend of medieval and modern Gothic, and fine eye for detail and craftsmanship, he added impact with an inspired use of vibrant colour. He once wrote that 'new work should look not different, but natural and harmonious'.

Light and airy, his quire with its limed-oak furnishings is given a high, pale blue patterned roof, with the magnificent organ case brilliantly painted in his favourite reds, greens, blues and gold.

The high altar is elegant and restrained with an attractive sunburst of wrought metalwork filling its Gothic arch backdrop. Of the small, intimate chapels on either side of the main altar, St Edmund's Chapel has an early 16th-century German painting as its reredos while the Transfiguration Chapel displays a poignant crucifix by the sculptor Dame Elisabeth Frink.

Seen throughout the cathedral, the individual kneelers were handcrafted in the 1960s. With the background colour based on the blue woollen cloth that brought great wealth to Suffolk during the Middle Ages, their designs represent every parish and many organisations in the diocese.

When Stephen Dykes Bower died in 1994 he left a legacy of £2 million in trust to the cathedral for continuing work on his original scheme and the completion of the north transept.

With a Millennium Commission grant and some serious fundraising in the late 1990s, the building of the lantern tower got underway. Like the great cathedrals of Peterborough (page 146) and Ely (page 68) it was built from Barnack stone in the traditional way with lime mortar.

On its completion, to notable acclaim, it seemed only fitting that a fine vaulted ceiling should be placed beneath the tower at the crossing. Made from oak and painted in exuberant fantailed bursts of gilded blue, green and red, it is a superb memorial to the man who brought St Edmundsbury Cathedral to vibrant life in the 21st century.

ST GILES' CATHEDRAL

The High Kirk of Edinburgh, Mother Church of Presbyterianism, St Giles' Cathedral is a powerful presence on Edinburgh's Royal Mile, its landmark crown spire beckoning visitors from afar. Standing centre stage at the heart of the city's historic Old Town, its story is inextricably linked with that of Scotland.

Only a few stones survive from the first church here, which was probably founded around 1124 by King David I. He had grown up in the Christian tradition thanks to his Anglo-Saxon mother, St Margaret, the pious Catholic queen of Malcolm III, King of Scots. It was dedicated to St Giles, the patron saint of cripples and lepers (and subsequently of Edinburgh itself) and given to the Lazarites, a religious order that cared for leprosy sufferers.

Fires and incursions by the English in the 14th century led to the rebuilding of the church in the Gothic style. The core of the current building dates from this time. It expanded almost haphazardly during the later medieval period, with chapels (known as aisles) being added to accommodate altars endowed by rich families and influential trade guilds. Dedicated to various saints and the Virgin Mary, there were around 50 side altars in St Giles' at the time of the Reformation, when all ties with Rome were severed.

The Kirk was at the heart of the Scottish Reformation and John Knox was at its head. A Scottish Catholic priest who converted to Protestantism in the 1540s, Knox spent many years in exile and while in Geneva was influenced by the French reformer, John Calvin.

On his return to Scotland in 1559, by this time a formidable orator, John Knox found the Reformed faith gaining ground. Marching an army of followers into St Giles', he preached there for the first time. A week later he was elected its minister, an office he held until his death in 1572.

The Scottish Parliament abolished papal authority in 1560 and Scotland officially became a Protestant country. All signs of Catholicism were stripped from the church, the stained-glass windows removed, treasures sold or melted down, the walls whitewashed. Over the years, partition walls were inserted to create separate areas where different congregations would gather around the preacher.

Following the 1603 Union of the Crowns, England and Scotland shared the same monarch but followed different forms of worship and church governance, with the Church of England retaining archbishops and bishops.

King Charles I's determination to bring the Scottish Church into line by creating a diocese in Edinburgh with St Giles the seat of its bishop – the only time the church has been a cathedral in the true meaning of the word – did not go down well. Nor did his insistence on imposing Anglican services on it.

Such was the fury that on Sunday 23 July, 1637, when Dean Hannay began reading from the new prayer book for the first time, a riot ensued, started, legend has it, when a local street trader named Jenny Geddes threw her stool at the Dean's head.

This incident led to the signing of the National Covenant, which called for religious freedoms and the independence of the Scottish Church, triggered the Bishops' Wars and eventually the Civil War. The Church of Scotland as we know it today was finally instituted in 1690.

By the 19th century St Giles' was in a bad state of repair, the true extent revealed when the tenements and shops built up against its walls, together with the Tolbooth that housed the infamous gaol, were demolished. Internally it was so divided that it contained four separate churches and even a police station.

The first period of restoration began in 1829 under architect William Burn, whose four years of work included demolishing some chapels, putting a focus on the cross shape of the cathedral and preserving the structure by encasing the outer walls in new sandstone.

The second phase, aimed at unifying and beautifying the building, took place between 1872 and 1883. It was planned and financed by the publisher and Lord Provost of Edinburgh, Sir William Chambers, whose vision was 'a Westminster Abbey for Scotland'.

The architect he chose, William Hay, removed all the internal partition walls to make the church one big space again. The best craftspeople of the time were employed to create the furnishings. Scottish sculptor John Rhind carved a new pulpit, font and statues for the improved west front. The acclaimed metalworker, Francis Skidmore, fashioned intricate railings for many side aisles (chapels).

Photo: Michael D Beckwith

Chambers died three days before the grand opening service but his nephew Robert continued the work, installing more monuments and memorials and introducing more stained glass.

The stained-glass windows are a highlight of St Giles', casting their glowing light over the serene interior. Many date from the Chambers restoration of the 1870s and show brilliantly detailed biblical scenes, often surmounted by hosts and choirs of angels.

There are some stunning windows by 20th-century and contemporary artists, too. Look especially at the north window designed by Douglas Strachan, full of dramatic colour as it portrays Jesus stilling the tempest, and don't miss the Robert Burns Window on the west wall. Designed by the Icelandic artist. Leifur Breidfjord, who also created the vibrant porch inside the main west entrance, it encapsulates the poet's life and work.

Set in neo-Gothic tracery, it begins with shades of green for the countryside, moves into blues and purples representing his belief in common humanity and rises to an explosion of red against a sunburst of yellow: Love above all.

Unusually, the Holy Table is placed at the very centre of the cathedral, at the crossing where the nave and transepts meet. The four massive pillars surrounding it, which support the tower and famed crown steeple, date from the 14th century and are hung with elegant modern banners, their colours changing with the ecclesiastical seasons.

Filled with memorials, each of the side aisles has a story to tell – so much of Scotland's history is revealed within these chapel walls that time spent exploring them will be well repaid.

The most modern addition to the structure of St Giles', the neo-Gothic Thistle Chapel, is spectacular. Built between

1909 and 1911, it is the spiritual home and meeting place of Scotland's order of chivalry: The Most Ancient and Most Noble Order of the Thistle.

Even the approach to it is impressive. Stepping down through decorative wrought iron gates you first enter a low-ceilinged room. Overhead are 57 stone-carved bosses and the walls are filled with countless dates and names of royalty, noblemen and knights going back to the founder, King James VII of Scotland (James II of England) in 1687. A narrow oak door beckons you into the chapel, where the vista of exquisite wood and stone carving stays long in the memory.

The 21st century has seen the 'renewal of St Giles', with the stained glass cleaned and conserved to reveal its vibrant colours and a new lighting scheme that has transformed the atmosphere of the church. Never in all its long history has St Giles' Cathedral looked so splendid.

ST KYNEBURGHA, CASTOR

Sometimes you find a church that appeals, stays long in the memory and becomes a favourite. The Church of St Kyneburgha in the leafy Cambridgeshire village of Castor is mine.

It's the only church known to be dedicated to the saint, a Saxon princess, erstwhile queen of Northumbria and daughter of Penda, the pagan King of Mercia. Her brothers built the original abbey at Peterborough (page 146) and in 650 Kyneburgha, together with her sister Kyneswitha, founded a convent in the Celtic tradition, with monks and

Photo: Marathon

nuns, on the ruins of a Roman palace. The Vikings sacked it in the 10th century.

Castor was a suburb of the sprawling Roman city of Durobrivae, spreading over the south bank of the River Nene and famed for its distinctive 'Castor Ware' pottery, which was exported throughout the empire. When the palace was built in AD 250, replacing a 1st-century villa, it was the second largest Roman building in Britain.

The Norman church was built over its courtyard; part of its temple lies under the Garden of Remembrance. Fragments of this long history, unearthed by those tending the gardens, are displayed in the church, alongside the stump of a pagan temple column re-used by the Saxons as the base for a cross.

Rare breed sheep are the official grass-mowers here, quite unfazed by the sloping terrain. Chosen because these breeds were known in the 12th century, which is when this lovely church was built, they're an appealing sight grazing between headstones and snoozing in the sun.

On a low hill, set back from the road and curtained by trees, St Kyneburgha's could be a textbook of medieval architecture. Dating from 1120 and built on Saxon foundations, it boasts arguably the finest Norman parish church tower in England, its two tiers of arcading impressively decorated and full of detailed carving. Many a cathedral would be envious of that workmanship.

Above the south porch a late-Saxon, stone-carved Christ in Majesty, flanked by the sun and moon, hands raised in blessing, beckons visitors into the Norman-arched entrance with its ancient and very heavy oak door. Inside all is light and cheering colour, graced by an angel roof; carved into the oak roof beams of the central nave, twelve brightly painted angels with outstretched gilded wings are clothed in colourful gowns. They carry musical instruments – pan pipes and violins, flutes, tambourines and mandolins – and represent the 'whole company of heaven'. The side aisles, too, have angel figures, regally bearing shields, books and musical instruments. Altogether there are over 60 of these angelic figures and they date from around 1450.

The sweeping Romanesque arches and sturdy clustered piers that line the nave have intriguing early-12th-century carved capitals. On the tower piers look for fighting men, birds, beasts and stylised foliage, St Kyneburgha seeing off men with evil intentions and several variations of the Green Man.

At the back of the north aisle, a 14th-century wall painting depicts scenes from the life of St Catherine. In the top panel she is seen converting some of the emperor's philosophers, the second panel shows them being executed and the third panel has St Catherine with the wheel that broke at her touch, when it was meant to kill her.

An 8th-century stone carving of St Mark that was probably on St Kyneburgha's original shrine stands by the altar dedicated to her sister, St Kyneswitha.

Beautifully stitched kneelers add much colour and interest to the pews. Talented locals also carved statues, made wrought iron light fittings and created the terracotta and slipware Stations of the Cross. Light, colourful, warm and welcoming, St Kyneburgha's feels a much-loved and cared-for parish church.

ST MAGNUS CATHEDRAL, KIRKWALL

Uniquely, Britain's most northerly cathedral belongs not to the Church but to the people of Orkney. King James III of

Scotland assigned its ownership to the city and community of Kirkwall in 1486, the year he elevated Kirkwall to the status of a royal burgh.

The Orkney Islands lie twelve miles (nineteen kilometres) off the north coast of Scotland, across the storm-swept Pentland Firth. Kirkwall, their capital and the principal town on the largest of the islands, known as the Mainland, grew out of a former Viking settlement and trading post. Probably founded in the 11th century, when the islands were under Norse rule, its name is derived from the Old Norse word *Kirkjuvagr*, meaning Church of the Bay.

Built with warm red sandstone and known as the 'Light in the North', St Magnus Cathedral dominates Kirkwall's skyline. It is a glorious example of Romanesque architecture and the best-preserved medieval cathedral in Scotland.

At the suggestion of his father, Kol, who supervised the initial building work, Earl Rögnvald founded the cathedral in memory of his uncle, the popular Earl Magnus. Murdered, (martyred, it is said), by his cousin and rival on the island of Egilsay where they'd met to resolve a dispute, he was canonised in 1135. When his bones were returned to Kirkwall and placed in a shrine, it became a place of pilgrimage and miracles were believed to have taken place there. The construction that had begun in 1137 continued for some 300 years.

The massive Norman pillars in the nave are reminiscent of those in Durham Cathedral (page 63) and indeed the original design for St Magnus was heavily influenced by that of Durham. The death of Earl Rögnvald in the 1150s brought construction to a standstill. A new, much larger plan had been envisaged by the time building restarted around 1190 and, given several extensions, it would take until the 15th century before it was completed.

Much of its warmth and appeal comes from the use of local red sandstone combined with yellow ochre sandstone for decorative effect. St Magnus may not be as big as the great English cathedrals, but its unity of style and the fine proportions of its graceful yet solid structure give it a sense of size that belies its actual dimensions.

Its interior is uncluttered, very much a place for worship, but there are several notable monuments to see and some good stained glass. There are memorials to two 19th-century Orcadian explorers, Dr John Rae, who charted much of the Canadian Arctic but never received the honours he deserved, and the missionary William Balfour Baikie who navigated up the Niger River and translated parts of the Bible into Hausa. The writer Eric Linklater spent many years in Orkney, identifying strongly with the islands of his father's birth. He is remembered here, as is the celebrated Stromness poet, George Mackay Brown.

Perhaps because it was under local ownership – maybe it was more difficult to desecrate the property of councillors, magistrates and the Kirkwall community – St Magnus didn't suffer as badly as most cathedrals in 1560 during the Reformation, although the organ, treasures and rich vestments were removed and the wall decorations covered in whitewash. A hundred years later, the building was damaged during Oliver Cromwell's siege when the Roundheads used the cathedral as a barracks and for stabling.

In the mid-19th century, the cathedral was in a very poor state of repair and major building restoration took place, but by the early 20th century it was again in bad shape. Thanks to a considerable bequest from Sheriff Thoms, who is commemorated in the fine east window, substantial renovations were carried out between 1919 and 1930.

Work included replacing the slated pyramid roof atop the

Photo: Stevekeiretsu

bell tower with a tall copper spire, the original having been struck by lightning in 1671; installing stained glass in the previously plain glass windows; and laying floor tiles based on medieval designs. It was at this time that the relics of St Magnus were discovered in a pillar in the quire. Rögnvald's relics, discovered at an earlier date, are in a pillar opposite. Finally the wonderful warm pink sandstone was again revealed, emerging from beneath layers of plaster and whitewash.

The east end of the quire was dedicated as St Rögnvald's Chapel in 1965. Carved figures representing Kol, Earl Rögnvald and Kirkwall's first bishop, Bishop William, were designed by the Kirkwall-born artist, Sir Stanley Cursiter.

The brilliant west window by Scottish stained-glass artist, Crear McCartney, is considered one of the finest contemporary windows in Scotland. Commissioned for the cathedral's 850th anniversary in 1987, it was entirely paid for by public subscription.

As well as hosting concerts and recitals throughout the year, the cathedral is a major venue for the St Magnus International Festival, a midsummer (June) celebration of the arts featuring world-class performances.

Next to the cathedral are the ruins of the former Bishop's Palace (12th century) and the Renaissance-style Earl's Palace. Don't miss the exhibits in the Orkney Museum across the way in historic Tankerness House, once a manse for cathedral clergy.

ST MARY THE VIRGIN, WELLINGBOROUGH

Tucked alongside a terrace of red-brick houses at the east end of an unremarkable East Midlands town, St Mary's appears to be an ordinary parish church, large but perhaps only of passing interest.

Appearances can be deceptive, however, for it was designed by Sir John Ninian Comper, one of the most influential and arguably the greatest among British church architects of the 20th century. The interior is sensational.

Comper considered St Mary's to be his finest work, certainly his favourite, and expressed his wish to be buried there with his wife. In the event, after his death in 1960 at the age of 96, such was his fame that his ashes were interred at Westminster Abbey – suitably placed beneath the windows he'd designed in the north aisle of the nave.

Entering under a severely plain, neatly crenellated tower of golden ironstone, nothing prepares you for the huge space, flooded with light, the amazing fan vaulting, the glorious gilded rood screen and the enveloping sense of calm to be found within. The plan is simple: Perpendicular Gothic with a broad nave, transept, chancel and two full-length side aisles with chapels attached. It's the design detail, the use of colour and the impact the church has on the visitor that makes it so special.

A committed Gothic Revivalist, Comper's journeys in Europe in the early 1900s led him to the conclusion that the beauty he sought to embody in Christian architecture need not be reliant on the medieval tradition but could incorporate the best of other architectural styles, too, and thus be universal. He called this drawing together 'unity by inclusion'. His other abiding belief was that a church should be functional. His was liturgy-driven architecture.

'The purpose of a church,' he wrote in 1917, 'is to move to worship, to bring a man to his knees, to refresh his soul in a weary land.'

Built between 1906 and 1931, and eventually consecrated

Photo: Sue Dobson

in 1968, St Mary's is a fine example of these ideals. Eight bays of tall, octagonal columns of warm local stone lead the eye through the ornate screen and gilded rood loft to the altar, reverently canopied by a gold-pillared ciborium, and finally the stained-glass windows shimmering in the distance. The simplicity of the nave's furnishings allows the most sacred parts of the church to leap instantly into focus.

Overhead, the highly decorated fan vaulting, its plaster dripping with pendants and studded with delicate bosses interlinked with snowflake-like roundels, feels surprisingly light in its whiteness. Stretching the entire length of the centre of the church, its detail is highlighted in gold and blue above both ends of the nave (baptismal font, high altar) and the screen – pinpointing their importance and offering an intimation of the vibrant colour that Comper originally planned for the whole church.

The classical worlds of Greece and Rome, the Italian Renaissance, English Gothic and medieval Byzantium all find their influences here.

The gloriously gilded rood screen with its gold and blue painted Tuscan columns and exquisitely decorated spandrels is surmounted by a filigree-fronted Gothic loft and crucifix, golden angels with scissor-folded wings and a fresh-faced Christ in Glory, the Pantocrator, ruler of all, presiding from on high.

Wrought iron screens, inspired by the *rejas* of Spanish cathedrals such as Seville, surround the sanctuary and are full of delightful Gothic Revival detail. The entwined initials of the three sisters, Gertrude, Harriet and Henrietta Sharman, the unmarried daughters of a local landowner, who in 1904 commissioned Ninian Comper to design a 'modest' church to serve the needs of the rapidly expanding town, appear on the screens closest to the high altar.

Painted with decorative garlands of blue flowers, the gilded Corinthian columns supporting the ciborium above the altar are topped with praying angels, with a sunburst of the Risen Christ at the canopy's centre. Impressive though this structure is, it hides some rather lovely stained glass in the window behind it. Comper used family and friends as models for his figures. The serene Virgin Mother and Child statue nearby have the features of his wife and son.

To the left of the sanctuary, the Holy Name of Jesus Chapel was the first part of the church to be completed and was dedicated in 1908. Here you get the full impact of Comper's flamboyant use of colour. The ceiling is panelled, painted in blue, dotted with Tudor roses and decorated with golden angels in full flight. The stained-glass window is a Tree of Jesse showing Christ's genealogy and the image of Mary, His mother, is modelled on a photograph of Grace Comper, Ninian's wife, whose ashes are buried here along with those of the architect's nephew and assistant, Arthur Bucknall, and his wife Ruth.

Over in the much simpler south chapel, dedicated to St John the Evangelist, some striking stained-glass windows depict men and women who suffered for their faith in different eras, from Katharine of Aragon to a set of Tractarian priests. Both chapels are in use for daily services, one for summer, one for winter.

Showing a Greek influence, the stone pillars rise in shades of the earth; the pleasing entwined vines and lily design of their capitals can be fully appreciated in the few that are painted. Comper's plan was for much more of the interior to be painted and gilded, but the money ran out, so we are tempted by what could have been by illustrative sections in colour, like the panelled aisle roofs patterned with black, red and white chevrons.

At the west end of the nave, the distinctive font and baptistry are magnificent, surrounded by an octagonal screen of carved and gilded dolphins and adorned with an elegant canopy. Sebastian, Ninian Comper's architect son, completed them as a memorial to his father.

This is an unexpected find in an unlikely setting. A vicar friend calls St Mary the Virgin in Wellingborough the finest parish church in England. He could be right.

ST PAUL'S CATHEDRAL, LONDON

For all the towering modern architecture that's risen around it in recent years, St Paul's Cathedral remains dominant; Wren's great dome is instantly recognisable as a symbol of London. Watching over Ludgate Hill, 24 steps leading up to its main entrance on the majestic west front, the cathedral stands above the crowd at the highest point within the Square Mile that constitutes the City of London. The world of business and banking spreads out beyond the building's eastern limits.

Mellitus, Bishop of the East Saxons, erected a wooden building here in 604 and there's been a cathedral dedicated to the Apostle St Paul on this site ever since. Fires and Viking attacks demolished the early churches but a vast and splendid construction, begun around 1087 under the conquering Normans, survived, despite many vicissitudes, for almost 600 years. Plans were afoot to restore the dilapidated medieval cathedral when the Great Fire of London in September 1666 changed everything. The catastrophic blaze, which destroyed two-thirds of the City of London including 13,200 houses and 87 parish churches, put it beyond repair.

Sir Christopher Wren – astronomer, scientist and mathematician, but much better remembered as a great architect – didn't have an easy time getting his plans for a new cathedral accepted. He produced his first design in 1669, but it took more designs and six years of wrangling before a decision was finally made. Royal approval, given by King Charles II for construction to begin in 1675, included the proviso that Wren could make adjustments when he deemed them necessary, a leeway he took to heart.

St Paul's was the first cathedral to be built in England after the Reformation and the first by a named architect. Wren lived to see the completion of his baroque masterpiece; in his declining years he was hauled up in a basket to oversee work on the roof. After its completion in 1711, he often returned to sit under the dome in contemplation. He died in 1723 and is buried in the cathedral's crypt. Part of the inscription in Latin on his simple tomb reads: 'Reader, if you seek his monument, look around you'.

The view as you enter from the west front is of a sweeping vista down the long nave, encompassing the full extent of this vast cathedral. Behind you are the nearly 30-foot- (nine-metre-) high Great West Doors, opened only on special occasions. The side aisles are lined with chapels and memorials, with the impressive monument to the Duke of Wellington, soldier, statesman and British military hero, placed in an arch between the nave and the north aisle.

St Paul's is built in the shape of a cross with, uniquely among English cathedrals, a dome crowning the intersection of its arms. Beneath it, the altar is encircled by seating for services. A highlight of a visit is to sit here and ponder the *trompe l'oeil* paintings high above, in which the figures, scenes and settings deceive the eye by appearing to be sculpted from stone. From 1715, the painter Sir James Thornhill spent the

Photo: Fanny-Margarita 22

next four years working on these monochrome murals based on the life of St Paul.

The triangular spaces in the spandrels between the arches of the crossing are filled with mosaics depicting four Old Testament prophets and the Evangelists Matthew, Mark, Luke and John. Designed by British artists, inspired by Roman art and created in a Venetian workshop, they were added in the mid- to late 19th century and are an introduction to the glorious mosaics to be seen in the quire and beyond.

Wren's iconic dome is a tour de force of engineering. At 365 feet (111 metres) high and weighing 65,000 tons, it is one of the largest cathedral domes in the world. Its innovative design consists of three distinct domes: the inner painted dome, the massive outer dome shell that dominated London's skyline and between the two, a brick cone that supports the ornate stone lantern above.

There are three gallery levels within this construction: around the inner painted dome, the quirkily acoustic whispering gallery is 252 steps up from the cathedral floor, while the stone gallery (376 steps up) and the golden gallery (528 steps up) encircle the outer dome and offer magnificent views across London for the fit and the brave with a head for heights.

In the 'arms' of the crossing, the highlight in the north transept is William Holman Hunt's painting *The Light of the World* (1900) and in the south transept, memorials to naval hero Horatio Nelson, artist J.M.W. Turner and Antarctic explorer Captain Robert Falcon Scott.

Ahead there's the quire, its canopied quire stalls exquisitely carved by Grinling Gibbons. The colourful mosaics covering the saucer domes of the ceiling depict the creation of the beasts of the earth, the fish of the sea and the birds of the air, seemingly supported by angels, arms aloft.

Covering the east end of the cathedral, the spectacular, vibrant mosaics were installed between 1894 and 1904 in response to Queen Victoria's complaint that St Paul's was 'dull, cold and dreary'. Shimmering in gold and glass, they were designed by the portrait artist William Blake Richmond, who had studied the art of mosaic in Italy, and tell Bible narratives from the Old and New Testaments.

High in the apse, the figure of Christ in Judgement, flanked by recording angels, watches over the modern (1958) high altar and ciborium (canopy) and the American Memorial Chapel, which commemorates those who lost their lives during the Second World War.

Below ground, the crypt stretches the entire length of the cathedral and contains tombs and memorials to the great, the good and the famous of the land. The marble sarcophagus on Lord Nelson's tomb had been intended for Cardinal Wolsey, King Henry VIII's Lord Chancellor, but after his fall from favour when he failed to arrange the king's divorce from Katharine of Aragon, it remained unused until a suitable recipient could be found. The crypt's intricately patterned mosaic flooring was the work of inmates of women's prisons around London.

SALISBURY CATHEDRAL

Salisbury Cathedral's elegant cream limestone spire, rising serenely above the water meadows of the River Avon, seems to epitomise England; its green lawns and the glorious close of elegant houses that surrounds it is probably the most famous of all cathedral closes. Constable was so enamoured that he sketched and painted the view some 300 times.

The Cathedral Church of the Blessed Virgin Mary, to give its full title, is unusual in that it was built in one style in a mere 38 years. The foundation stones were laid in 1220, three altars in the first chapels to be completed were dedicated five years later and the cathedral was consecrated in 1258, with the west front, cloisters and chapter house finished a few years after that. Being English Gothic through and through gives it an austere simplicity and purity of line that has attracted as many critics as enthusiasts.

In the nave, tall slim columns, defined with dark shafts of Purbeck Marble, and layers of pointed arches all seem to rise heavenwards. The view down the nave is of the entire length of the cathedral, an unobstructed vista encompassing the high altar and beyond to the Trinity Chapel at the east end.

After entering through the porch of the pale stone and statue-filled west front, your first thought may be that dullness seems to pervade the interior. But look back down the nave from the quire, and you get a very different, positively uplifting vision.

The nave's spectacular centrepiece is the huge Living Water font, designed by the multi-award-winning British water sculptor William Pye. It was installed in 2008 as part of the celebrations that marked the 750th anniversary of the cathedral's consecration.

Composed of a bronze vessel above a base of Purbeck stone, its still surface water reflects the surrounding architecture and flows serenely in an endless movement through spouts at the four pointed corners, to disappear through a bronze grating on the floor. It is mesmerizingly beautiful.

The north nave aisle holds a model of the cathedral during construction and the world's oldest working mechanical clock, dating back to medieval 1386. Designed only to strike the hour, it has no face. Originally housed in the freestanding bell tower, which was severely damaged during the English Civil War and subsequently demolished, it chimed the hours for centuries.

At the crossing you can see how the weight of the tower and spire (about 6,500 tons) has distorted the supporting marble columns. There's a hole in the lierne-vaulted ceiling through which building materials were hauled up into the tower by a wooden windlass. That is still where the builders left it, as is the oak scaffolding installed as reinforcement after a storm in 1360.

Salisbury's famous octagonal spire was added in the early 14th century. An extraordinary feat of engineering, it soars to 404 feet (123 metres) and is the tallest in Britain. To help support the piers below, two great strainer arches of carved stone were added to the crossing in the 15th century.

There are more strainer arches in the quire transepts, each with an inverted 'scissor' arch of wonderfully sinuous lines. They present a stunning backdrop to the 106 oak quire stalls, which are original, some of them a gift from the pious King Henry III in 1236. Their canopies are Victorian, with those over the rear stalls containing statues of bishops of Salisbury.

The Trinity Chapel lies behind the high altar. As you walk there, don't miss the revolving glass prism in the Morning Chapel, off the north quire aisle. Showing scenes in and around the cathedral, it was engraved by Sir Laurence Whistler as a memorial to his brother, the artist Rex Whistler, who lived in the close and died leading troops in Normandy in 1944. An exquisite work of art, it is set into what remains of the 13th-century carved stone quire screen that was removed during some fairly disastrous 'restoration' work towards the end of the 18th century.

Photo: Tony Hisgett

You'll also pass the magnificent carved stone Audley Chantry Chapel. Built for Edmund Audley, who was Bishop of Salisbury from 1502 to 1524, and placed alongside the high altar, it is a superb example of the Perpendicular style of architecture. Still retaining some of its original colour, the fan-vaulted ceiling includes a vandalised image of the Virgin Mary within the Bishop's emblem and the red roses of King Henry VIII linked with pomegranates, the emblem of his first wife, Queen Katharine of Aragon.

The powerful and intricate Prisoners of Conscience Window dominates the Trinity Chapel at the east end. Installed in 1980, it pays homage to people of all races and faiths who suffer persecution for their beliefs and was designed and made by Gabriel and Jacques Loire, a father and son team, in their workshop in Chartres. The Amnesty International candle burns nearby.

Salisbury was never a monastic foundation but its cloisters are among the largest in England. Completed around 1266 and designed for processions, they enclose a peaceful garden shaded by two cedars of Lebanon planted in honour of Queen Victoria's accession to the throne in 1837.

The entrance to the chapter house is off the east side of the cloister. Octagonal in shape and dating from the mid-13th century, its fan-vaulted ceiling rises voluptuously from a single central column. Stone bench seats for the canons are set into the walls, with raised seats for the bishop, dean and dignitaries. Above them a frieze depicts scenes from the first two books of the Bible. Look for Noah's Ark shaped like a Viking ship.

This is the setting for an interactive exhibition proudly presenting the cathedral's copy of the Magna Carta. In the best condition of the four originals surviving from 1215, its 3,500 words are written in abbreviated Latin on a single piece of vellum. Explanations of its origins and importance, also its association with people involved in the building of the cathedral, are given on well-designed storyboards.

In 1445, the bishop and chapter built a library over the eastern cloister. Originally twice its present length, it contains many ancient manuscripts including a page of the Old Testament in Latin from the 8th century.

Most towns grew up around the central point of worship, for example monastic Peterborough (page 146) and Malmesbury (page 131), but here in Salisbury the town was built at the same time as the cathedral. The close with its fine stone houses for the canons and clergy was edged on the north and east sides by streets that crossed at right angles to form 'chequers'. The core of this medieval 'new town' can still be discerned.

By the 13th century Salisbury had become a noted centre of learning, a tradition that has continued. Sarum College, a former theological college, is today an ecumenical centre for Christian study and research and the crenellated Bishop's Palace is the main building of Salisbury Cathedral School.

Pausing to admire Dame Elizabeth Frink's bronze 'Walking Madonna', cross the manicured lawns of the close, such an integral part of the cathedral ensemble, to explore a cluster of excellent museums in beautiful settings.

There's the award-winning Salisbury Museum in The King's House and the delightful Mompesson House (National Trust), the perfect example of a Queen Anne House set in a peaceful garden. Arundells was the home of former Prime Minister, Sir Edward Heath and exhibits a fascinating collection that reflects his life in politics and interests from sailing to music and fine art.

Do walk by the river for views of the cathedral that Constable would still recognise.

SHERBORNE ABBEY

The Abbey Church of St Mary the Virgin was first a Saxon cathedral, then a Benedictine abbey and since the dissolution of the monasteries, a parish church. Affectionately referred to as 'the cathedral of Dorset', its stunning fan vaulting makes it one of the most spectacular parish churches in an English market town.

St Aldhelm was Abbot of Malmesbury Abbey (page 131) in 705 when the Diocese of Sherborne was created. Encompassing what are now the counties of Dorset, Somerset and Wiltshire, Aldhelm was appointed its bishop, the first Bishop of the West Saxons.

It is quite possible that his decision to build a church at Sherborne was influenced by the existence of an earlier Celtic community on the site, but nothing remains of that, or indeed of his cathedral. Situated close to the west end of the current abbey, it was probably quite small, but given his connections to the Wessex royal family, likely to have been richly furnished.

The cathedral was enlarged, served 26 Saxon bishops after Aldhelm, and had a monastery built around it. In 998 the 20th bishop, St Wulfsin, ejected the existing community of secular canons and invited monks of the Order of St Benedict to serve it, making himself their first abbot. Then in 1075 the new Norman rulers transferred the bishopric to Old Sarum, near present day Salisbury, which meant that Sherborne lost its status as a cathedral.

The Norman builders got to work on rebuilding the abbey in Romanesque style in around 1140. Remnants of this period are still visible in the rounded arches at the tower crossing and interlaced arcading in side chapels. The dogtooth carvings you pass on entering the church are also Norman, the porch having been added in around 1180.

It was the great rebuilding of 1380 to 1500, when pretty much everything Romanesque got covered over in the Perpendicular style, that gave us the pointed arches, the huge windows and most of all, the glorious fan vaulting so much admired today.

Sherborne's fan vaulting, among the earliest in England on such a scale, covers almost the whole church. Note how the fans are complete semicircles and don't overlap or cut into one another, unlike the later, more complicated patterns seen for example in King's College Chapel, Cambridge (page 112). Their starbursts meet in the centre and display some superb medieval stone-carved bosses (binoculars come in handy here) – 115 of them in the nave alone.

The colourfully ornate roof above the quire, where the fans come closer to touching, seems even more spectacular. The vaulting in the north transept is different again, its bosses appearing larger and more flowery, their colourings reflected in the decorative pipes within the carved wood organ case below.

All was not well between the town's inhabitants and the abbey monks during the 15th century. Among the locals' many grievances was being forced to use All Hallows, a small church (or rather 'chapel of ease') tacked on to the abbey building, for their worship and having to go cap in hand to the abbot to use the Abbey's font when they wanted their children baptised.

The feuding came to a head in 1437 when the townspeople installed their own font and the enraged Abbot sent 'a stout butcher' armed with a hammer to break it up. A riot ensued, during which a burning arrow shot into wooden scaffolding caused a massive blaze and much destruction.

It took the intervention of the Pope to settle the conflict, the result being that the people had to pay for the reconstruction! It cost them dearly, for only the finest builders and masons were employed and it took 50 years to complete.

There must have been some happy people when, in 1539, Abbot John Barnstaple and his sixteen monks surrendered Sherborne to King Henry VIII's commissioners. Thanks to Sir John Horsey, the local wheeler-dealer MP and Privy Councillor under Thomas Cromwell, who wanted the abbey's extensive lands and property but not its church, the Abbey was sold off to the townspeople for use as their parish church. They immediately demolished All Hallows.

Not that they got the Abbey for nothing. Sir John, who made a fortune from the dissolution, charged the town £350 (the equivalent of tens of millions pounds today) despite the fact that between him and the commissioners the church had been stripped bare of its treasures.

Later, under the Protestant laws of the 16th century, its walls were whitewashed and the Lady Chapel sold off. Remodelled in 1560, the chapel became the three-storey house of the headmaster of King Edward VI's new grammar school (now Sherborne School).

Consequently, when Cromwell's soldiers invaded in 1645 there was little left to damage, though they did deface Sir John Horsey's elaborate tomb. It was the Victorian restoration, begun in 1850 and lasting for eight years, which brought the Abbey back to glorious life. Out went the box pews, galleries and other impedimenta; in came colour and a long unimpeded view to the raised altar.

Ten medieval misericords survive under the seats of the

back stalls in the Victorian canopied quire. One depicting a schoolboy being caned is so detailed that even the welts in his bottom are displayed.

The great east window is from the mid-19th century and tells the story of the Passion of Christ. The elaborate tracery lights above are filled with images of saints and the Four Evangelists. Two are of local Celtic saints, Sidwell and her sister Juthware, both martyred and greatly venerated in medieval Sherborne.

The fine Caen stone altar reredos on the altar, depicting the Ascension of Christ into Heaven, was carved by the English Gothic Revival architect, Richard Herbert Carpenter. His other memorable feat at Sherborne was to restore the 15th-century tower, which holds the heaviest peal of eight church bells in the world. The massive tenor bell, weighing in at over two tons, was a gift from Cardinal Wolsey.

The little Lady Chapel at the east end is now a fraction of its original size. Returned by Sherborne School and restored in the 1930s, in its stained-glass windows are scenes from the early history of the Abbey, including St Aldhelm presenting a model of his cathedral to its patron, the Virgin Mary. Laurence Whistler, the celebrated glass engraver, designed the unusual reredos behind the altar in 1968. His engraved prism in memory of his artist brother Rex features in Salisbury Cathedral (page 197).

At the east end of the north aisle, look for the brass plate that indicates Alfred the Great's younger brothers, Ethelbald and Ethelbert, both kings in their own right, were buried in the Abbey in the 9th century. Tradition holds that Alfred himself was educated at the monastery here. All 38 known colours (battle standards) of the Dorsetshire Regiment hang along this aisle. Dating back to 1800, each one has a framed history.

Photo: MikeofDorset

In the south transept, the Te Deum Window is an Augustus Pugin design from 1850. The main lights have 96 figures of Apostles, prophets and martyrs and above them are 31 angels, seraphim and cherubim proclaiming 'Sanctus'. Although faded, it is still impressive.

It shines down on the massive, ornately baroque monument to John Digby, third Earl of Bristol, flanked by his two wives. Digby, whose main claim to fame was that he allowed William of Orange and his forces to land in Devon to begin the Glorious Revolution against the Catholic King James II, commissioned his own memorial eleven years before his death in 1698. From his demeanour, you might feel that it's more of a monument to his wealth and ego.

Sir Walter Raleigh is said to have worshipped in the next chapel, dedicated to St Katharine, which contains the Abbey's remaining medieval glass. A small collection, mostly dating from the 15th century, it was arranged in 1925 and includes Yorkist and Lancastrian roses, crowns, heads, shields and monograms of Christ and the Virgin Mary.

The great west window, made by the British stained-glass artist, John Hayward, was installed in 1997. Its theme is the Incarnation and at its centre the Blessed Virgin Mary is seated among the branches of a tree, with the Christ Child on her lap. Very thoughtfully designed, it links the Old and New Testaments and repays a careful look.

It was dedicated in 1998 in the presence of Queen Elizabeth II and the Duke of Edinburgh, a moment that is recalled in the same artist's Millennium Window, which reflects on the thousand years since the arrival of the Benedictines at Sherborne Abbey in 998.

Set within a small close edged by houses, which, like the abbey and old town, were built from the warm local sandstone, Sherborne Abbey remains a much-loved parish church. It is also a popular venue for concerts and hosts an award-winning music festival every year in May.

SOUTHWARK CATHEDRAL

On the south bank of the River Thames, surrounded by trendy Borough Market and the cloud-piercing peaks of The Shard, Southwark Cathedral stands firm, a sanctuary amid a chaotic swirl of railway bridges, skyscrapers and a tide of City workers making their way across nearby London Bridge. Designated a cathedral in 1905 when the Anglican Diocese of Southwark was formed, much of its long history is revealed by its full title: the Cathedral and Collegiate Church of St Saviour and St Mary Overie, Southwark.

There may have been a Roman temple here – a statue of a Roman hunter god was discovered during excavations – and legends tell that there was a Saxon convent on the site, replaced by a college of canons founded by Bishop Swithun of Winchester (page 245). However, the first written reference appeared in the Domesday Book of 1086, to a 'minster' headed by Bishop Odo of Bayeux, the half-brother of William the Conqueror.

Refounded by two Norman knights in 1106 as an Augustinian priory dedicated to the Virgin Mary, its church was named St Mary Overie (over-the-river). The Bishops of Winchester, in whose diocese Southwark lay, built a magnificent palace nearby and used St Mary Overie as their church.

Burned down in the great fire that swept through Southwark and crossed London Bridge in 1212, it was rebuilt

Photo: Amandajm

in the latest Early English architectural style, making it London's first Gothic church.

The Augustinian Canons, who would have welcomed pilgrims on their way to Canterbury, built a hospital at the priory gates dedicated to St Thomas Becket. This was the foundation of London's renowned St Thomas' Hospital, transferred to its present location opposite the Houses of Parliament in 1871.

Outside the jurisdiction of the City of London across the river, Southwark was a dangerous place, known for its gambling dens, brothels, overcrowded lodging houses and the notorious Clink and Marshalsea prisons. The Canons were forbidden to leave the priory unaccompanied.

The monastery was dissolved under King Henry VIII in 1539 but the church survived and was renamed St Saviour's. An agreement that the congregation could rent it from the Crown lasted until a group of merchants who worshipped there, known as 'the Bargainers', bought the church from King James I for £800.

With the Globe Theatre nearby, St Saviour's would have been William Shakespeare's parish church. His younger actor brother, Edmund, was buried here (in 1607) as were the influential dramatists John Fletcher (1625) and Philip Massinger (1640). A stained-glass window and several memorials celebrate the theatrical traditions of the church.

Built between 1220 and 1420, although the cathedral retains its basic Gothic structure there have been many additions, repairs and reconstructions down the centuries.

By the 19th century it was in a ruinous state and narrowly avoided being demolished when proposals were made for a wider approach to London Bridge. The vast railway viaduct that was built in 1852 passes just eighteen metres from the south-east corner of the cathedral.

With the decision made to restore the fabric, local architect George Gwilt the Younger came to the rescue, saving the tower and the east end of the church. In 1890, Sir Arthur Blomfield, who had earlier designed the Royal College of Music in South Kensington, was appointed to rebuild the nave.

He did so in the Gothic style of the original 13th-century church, replicating its alternating round and square piers, giving a clear sightline to the cathedral's greatest treasure, the ornate altar screen. Erected in 1520, it is very similar in style to that at Winchester Cathedral.

Its niches were restored in 1833, after a covering wooden screen installed by the Puritans and inscribed with the Ten Commandments, the Creed and the Lord's Prayer, was removed. The statues were added in the early 20th century and depict people with an historical connection to Southwark.

With Christ the Saviour as the central figure they include saints, martyrs and kings, as well as numerous bishops of Winchester. One of them, Cardinal Archbishop Henry Beaufort, installed the cathedral bells for the wedding of his niece Joan to King James I of Scotland in 1424.

To the right of the great screen is the painted effigy tomb of Lancelot Andrewes who died in 1626. Bishop of Winchester and Master of Pembroke College, Cambridge he was one of the main translators of the King James Bible (also known as the Authorised Version).

Behind it is the retroquire, a lovely space with slim columns and graceful arches. Used as a courtroom by the Winchester bishops, it was here that in 1555, during the reign of Queen Mary I, Bishop Stephen Gardiner conducted a heresy trial that sent six high-ranking clergymen, including the Bishop of Gloucester and the Bishop of St Davids, to their deaths, burned at the stake.

The four chapels were furnished in 1930 by Sir Ninian Comper (who designed the lovely Church of St Mary the Virgin in Wellingborough, page 188). His stained-glass window depicting Christ in Majesty flanked by the Virgin Mary, St John and a fluttering of doves, is set above the great screen in the quire.

In the north aisle, a window depicts Chaucer's pilgrims setting off for Canterbury from Southwark's Tabard Inn. Nearby is the colourful and elaborate canopied tomb of Chaucer's good friend John Gower, court poet to King Richard II and King Henry IV, who in his later life lived in the Augustinian priory precincts. He is depicted with his head supported by his three main works, books written in French, Latin and English.

Across the nave, William Shakespeare is immortalised in sculptor Henry McCarthy's 1912 alabaster statue, depicted reclining on his elbow and framed by decorative stone carving. A stained-glass window depicts scenes from his plays and a memorial tablet honours Sam Wanamaker, the driving force behind the construction of Shakespeare's Globe Theatre on Bankside.

Other windows to look for are the three lancets to the west by the Pre-Raphaelite artist Henry Holiday, which display the story of the Creation; Sir Ninian Comper's Christ the Healer in the north quire aisle; and the Rider Window by Lawrence Lee in the retroquire. Telling of the building and rebuilding of Southwark Cathedral, it was given by the family of Thomas Rider whose firm rebuilt the nave in the 1890s. Next to it, the Icelandic artist Leifur Breidfjord's abstract design, 'celebration of life', was installed to mark the Queen's Diamond Jubilee in 2012.

Off the north transept, the Harvard Chapel commemorates John Harvard, the Southwark-born minister who immigrated to Massachusetts and was baptised in this church in 1607. Funded by alumni of the university that bears his name, its window depicts the Baptism of Christ, with the arms of Emmanuel College, Cambridge, where John Harvard studied, and those of Harvard University. The tabernacle is a towering, jewel-studded masterpiece by the Gothic Revival architect Augustus Pugin.

Two disasters have happened on the cathedral's doorstep: the sinking of the *Marchioness* pleasure boat under Southwark Bridge in 1989 and the attack on Borough Market in 2017. The 51 people who drowned on the *Marchioness* have a touching memorial while PC Wayne Marques GM, a first-responder injured during the terrorist attack, is depicted on a new replacement corbel (as is one of Southwark Cathedral's most famous inhabitants, the stray cat who stayed and was named Doorkins Magnificat).

On the site of the original cloisters, an innovative and award-winning new development, opened in 2001 by Nelson Mandela, includes a café and shop. The churchyard was restored in 2015 and planted with flowers and herbs with biblical and Shakespearean connections. Moving with the times, Southwark Cathedral is very much a part of the local community.

TEWKESBURY ABBEY

One of the largest parish churches in England, Tewkesbury's Abbey Church of St Mary the Virgin was consecrated in 1121 and replaced a Saxon church and monastery. A consecration cross can still be discerned in the stone to the left of the entrance.

The nave speaks of Norman power and might. Fourteen gigantic drum columns, each six and a half feet (almost two metres) wide and a towering 30 feet (nine metres) tall support an intricate lierne vaulting that's one of the finest roofs to be created in the early 14th century.

In the Decorated Gothic style, its ribs flow effortlessly from the pier capitals, meeting, intersecting and linked by remarkably detailed carved stone bosses. The fifteen in the centre line depict events in the life of Christ, from the Nativity to the Crucifixion, the Resurrection to Christ in Glory. Surrounding smaller images are of winged angels, many playing musical instruments. All are painted and gilded.

There's a splendid view of the great columns, rounded arches and lierne vaulting from the quire, framed by the lacy, carved oak rood screen that separates it from the nave.

The quire sits under the tower, a fine collection of misericords under its stalls. On the floor, a brass plate marks the burial place of Edward, the Lancastrian Prince of Wales, slain during the Battle of Tewkesbury in 1471. Overhead, the lierne vaulting displays colourful blue and red emblems. King Edward IV had the gilded and glittering Suns of York set in the roof after the Yorkist victory in that bloody battle.

The Milton organ, one of the oldest still in use and quite recently restored, was originally built for Magdalene College, Oxford in 1631 and bought for the Abbey in 1737. John Milton, the learned 17th-century poet and polemicist, is reputed to have played it.

Steps lead up to simple high altar of Purbeck Marble. On its south side are the remains of an ancient three-seater sedilia, used by the clergy during services, still with some of its original colouring in the carved stone. Look up to the right to see the statue of the kneeling knight in a filigree tower. It's an effigy of Lord Edward le Despenser in full armour and sits atop his chantry chapel in the south quire aisle.

In the Middle Ages, three important families held the 'Honour of Tewkesbury': the de Clares, the le Despensers and Richard Neville, Earl of Warwick (known as 'Warwick the King-Maker'). Local aristocracy with powerful royal connections, generations of their members were buried in the Abbey.

After her husband Hugh le Despenser, a favourite of Edward II, was hanged in Hereford in 1326, Eleanor de Clare embarked on a massive rebuilding of the quire and ambulatory, which would contain the elaborate chantry chapels of her noble dynasty. It was she who gave the glorious windows containing very fine examples of 14th-century English stained glass.

Eleanor's son Hugh and his wife Elizabeth de Montacute lie in alabaster splendour beneath an exquisitely fashioned canopy, its tiers of open tracery rising almost to the vault arch above.

Erected in 1422 by Isabelle le Despenser to the memory of her first husband, Richard Beauchamp, whose bravery at Agincourt gained him the title Earl of Worcester, the impressive Warwick Chapel has two storeys, intricately patterned stonework and filigree carving so fine it resembles lace.

At the dissolution, when Abbot John Wakeman and his Benedictine monks surrendered to the Crown in 1540, Tewkesbury was one of the richest abbeys in England. The list of its possessions filled 74 skins of parchment. Abbot Wakeman was rewarded – he was made the first Bishop of Gloucester.

Photo: Paul Pichota

The monastery buildings and the large Lady Chapel were pulled down and used, near and far, for building stone. The sum of £453 was considered the value of the remaining lead and bells, had they been melted down. The townspeople paid and continued using the western part of the Norman nave as their parish church.

There are several chapels within the church but don't miss the Chapel of St Catherine and St John the Baptist off the north quire aisle at the east end. Its windows were designed by the contemporary stained-glass artist Tom Denny, whose work is also seen in the cathedrals at Hereford (page 101) and Gloucester (page 88).

Installed in 2002 to mark the 900th anniversary of the Benedictine monks coming to Tewkesbury, their colours are in vibrant shades of greens, blues and golden yellows. The abstract design is based on the Benedictine motto *Laborare est Orare* (to work is to pray).

Even the Abbey's shop is in a 13th-century chapel. It was the burial place of the Lancastrian leaders, executed by the Yorkists after the great battle of 1471, and for 300 years until the 1870s was used as a grammar school.

Watching over Tewkesbury town, the Abbey's square Norman tower dominates the landscape for miles around. With its zigzag decoration, blind arcading and corner turrets, it is considered among the largest and finest of Romanesque towers in England. A corona of chapels surrounds the east end of the building while the west front is dominated by a vast Norman recessed arch 65 feet (twenty metres) high and 34 feet (ten metres) wide. Outside and inside, Tewkesbury Abbey presents much to admire.

TINTERN ABBEY

Set in a peaceful valley amid tree-covered hills on the Welsh bank of the meandering River Wye, the ruins of Tintern Abbey have inspired poets from Wordsworth and Tennyson to Alan Ginsberg. J.M.W. Turner painted the atmospheric scene several times, with some dramatic depictions of the ivy-covered site.

Tintern Abbey was the first Cistercian monastery in Wales (and only the second in Britain). It was founded in 1131 by Walter fitz Richard de Clare, the Anglo-Norman Lord of Chepstow, and prospered from large endowments of land in Gloucestershire and Monmouthshire.

The first monks came from the Norman abbey of L'Aumône and before long attracted many local novices, mainly of Anglo-Norman or English origin. They were so successful that within eight years they were able to colonise a 'daughter house' at Kingswood in Gloucestershire. Then in 1203, a group of monks travelled to Ireland to found Tintern Parva (Little Tintern) near Wexford.

The Cistercian Order that flourished in France during the 12th and 13th centuries spread rapidly across Britain. It demanded strict observance of the original ascetic Rule of St Benedict, the plan for monastic community life compiled by Benedict of Nursia in the 6th century.

Poverty, simplicity, prayer, obedience and manual work were their watchwords. Cistercian abbeys were to be sited in isolated locations, their churches plain and unadorned. The monks wore habits made from coarse undyed wool, their vegetarian diet was meagre and they were bound by a strict rule of silence.

Photo: Niftanion

Agriculture was crucial to their existence and the educated choir monks were joined by large numbers of illiterate lay brothers who cleared and cultivated the land. The extensive estates given by rich landowners were organised into compact farms known as granges.

As the monastery grew in numbers and wealth, building activity was a constant. Modest wooden structures probably greeted the first monks on their arrival. A small stone Romanesque church together with stone monastic buildings appeared some years later. The major expansion came in the 13th century with a new refectory, monks' dormitories, a large infirmary and extended cloisters.

The great Abbey Church was rebuilt in the Gothic style between 1269 and 1301 under the patronage of Roger Bigod III, fifth Earl of Norfolk, Lord of Chepstow and at the time one of the most powerful men in the court of King Edward I. Completion of the church and its furnishings continued for several decades into the 14th century, when the abbot's residence was extended in grand style.

Much of the early austerity that had defined the Cistercian way of life had fallen away by this time. Meat had been introduced into the monks' diet and they were allowed more space and comforts in their surroundings. Changes were also afoot in the matter of agriculture and sources of funds.

Roger Bigod's grant of manorial lands in Norfolk and Gloucestershire brought an impressive income, as did tithes from a church in Kent. More and more land was being leased out to tenants for cash rents. The ideals of grange farming were already being abandoned when the Black Death plague of 1349 greatly diminished the number of lay brothers, leaving the abbey with a severe labour shortage.

By the 15th century the isolation once demanded of a Cistercian monastery had also gone by the board. The homes, workplaces, shops and taverns of a settled local community nudged right up to the high walls of the abbey precinct.

The monastery was dissolved in 1536 when Abbot Wyche surrendered it to King Henry VIII's commissioners. The abbot and twelve remaining choir monks received pensions; valuables were carted off to the King's Treasury and within a few months the abbey buildings and lands were granted to Henry Somerset, Earl of Worcester.

In later years, furnaces, forges and mills turned the site into an industrial complex. The monastic buildings fell into ruinous decay, their debris colonised by brambles, but the Abbey Church, although roofless after being stripped of its lead and with its windows smashed, seems to have withstood the ravages of time rather better. In the 18th century, locals were using it for playing quoits and the ball game, fives.

With the rise of Romanticism towards the end of that century, tourists began discovering the wild beauty of the Wye Valley. The Reverend William Gilpin's guidebook, *Observations on the River Wye*, became an immediate bestseller when it was published in 1782.

They travelled down the river in small boats, complete with sketchbooks and picnic hampers, keen to reach Tintern Abbey, which Gilpin described as the most beautiful scene of all. A new road built in the 1820s and the arrival of the Wye Valley Railway in 1876 made the ivy-clad ruins more accessible for the ever-increasing number of Victorian visitors.

In 1901, recognised as a monument of national importance, Tintern was purchased by the Crown and F. W. Waller, architect to Gloucester Cathedral, was engaged to supervise conservation work on the fragile structure. A massive undertaking, the restoration scheme was to last for nearly 30 years.

The best-preserved medieval abbey in Wales, Tintern is now in the care of Cadw, the historic environment service of the Welsh Government, which continues to carry out conservation projects, most recently on the celebrated 13th-century west front.

A great glory of the Abbey Church is its window tracery and the patterning of the huge central window on the west front is particularly impressive. With seven lights it soars gracefully, a fine example of the fashionable Decorated style. Its sheer scale dominates the main entrance doorway below, which has trefoil-headed openings set between equally decorative paired niches.

The plan of the church is a simple cruciform with an aisled nave of six bays, a still impressive sight of sturdy clustered piers and arcades of sharply pointed Gothic arches. The internal divisions have long gone, but the nave, reserved for the lay brothers, would have been separated from the quire and presbytery, the preserve of the choir monks, at the east end. The aisles, too, designed as passageways, would have been walled off, lit by windows in each of the bays. The red-brown sandstone walls were originally plastered in white lime and the floor covered by glazed and patterned clay tiles.

Look for rich window tracery in the bay at the east end of the north aisle. Below it the processional doorway, used by the choir monks entering the church from the cloister, has some sumptuous carving and decorative detail.

The moulding on the arches in the monks' quire is more elaborate than that seen in the nave. A richly decorated pulpitum originally divided the monks from the lay brothers but the Victorians disposed of it around 1880. The great east window has lost its tracery and now opens onto a fine view of wooded hills. At the crossing, four immense arches rise from massive multi-clustered piers and each transept contained two chapels.

Little remains of the cloister, the chapter house or the ranges of the monastic buildings, but it is still possible to see the layout of the precinct and the chambers where monks lived, worked and prayed for nigh on four centuries. The setting, an Area of Outstanding Beauty, is lovely and the Gothic abbey, open to the skies, is one of Wales' special places.

TRURO CATHEDRAL

The Cathedral Church of the Blessed Virgin Mary in Truro may appear medieval, but it was built between 1880 and 1910 by some very fine Victorian craftspeople. In the Early English Gothic style of the 13th century, with its three spires it is a focal point at the heart of the city.

When the new Anglican diocese to serve Cornwall was created in 1876, Truro's cathedral was the first to be built on a new site in Britain since Salisbury Cathedral (page 197) in the early 13th century.

The architect was John Loughborough Pearson, a scholar of French Gothic and keen evangelical who considered that a cathedral should 'send you to your knees'. He died while it was still being constructed and the project was taken over by his architect son, Frank Loughborough Pearson, who also completed his father's plans for St Matthew's Church in Auckland, New Zealand, which is very similar in style to Truro Cathedral.

In a poor state of repair, the medieval parish church of St Mary was demolished to make way for the cathedral, but the architect insisted that its south aisle be incorporated into his new building. Known as St Mary's Aisle, it still functions as the city centre's parish church.

Built from Cornish granite, with creamy Bath stone providing the decorative detail, the overall effect is impressive. In a profusion of piers, columns and arcades of arches sharply pointed and gently rounded, the long rib-vaulted nave draws the eye to the remarkable stone-carved reredos dominating the high altar. The biblical scenes are so detailed, the faces so expressive, it is a triumph of craftsmanship by the British architectural sculptor, Nathaniel Hitch.

The Way of the Cross is superb, too. This large terracotta frieze, crowded with lifelike characters, full of movement and the finest detail, was the work of George Tinworth.

Born into extreme poverty, Tinworth became Royal Doulton's most important designer of decorative vases and humorous pottery figures. There he was held in such esteem that he was given his own studio and allowed to take on outside commissions, exhibiting his biblical scenes at the Royal Academy to great acclaim.

Truro's highlight and true glory, however, must be the stained-glass windows. Made entirely by the London firm of Clayton & Bell, famed for their use of strong, jewel-like colour and ability to tell biblical stories in the medieval style, it was the largest stained-glass project ever made. Inspired by the architect's love of European cathedrals, the scheme incorporated three large rose windows that portray the Holy Trinity.

God the Father is at the heart of the Creation rose window: *Fiat Lux*, let there be light; the north transept rose depicts God the Son and the genealogy of Christ; a dove, representing God the Holy Spirit is at the centre of the south transept rose and tells of Pentecost. A window of

Christ in Majesty at the end of time dominates the east end of the building.

In the windows, a total of 104 lights encompass the fundamental Christian beliefs, Old Testament history and the Gospel narratives. The development of 1,900 years of Christianity is represented by 108 historic individuals and significant events, from St Peter 'upon this rock I will build my church' to the laying of the foundation stone of Truro Cathedral. Many are specifically related to Cornwall, its saints, preachers and the livelihoods of its people. The detail in each one is extraordinary.

Although all the windows were paid for by donors, they did not get a say in the content or design, which is not only unusual, it is probably unique. All but two windows in the north nave aisle were in place by 1913. The last two lancets were inserted in 1938, made by Clayton & Bell and largely to the original design.

The whole, grand, integrated scheme for the windows was created in a close collaboration between the first Bishop of Truro, the much-admired Edward White Benson, and the architect J.L. Pearson.

The bishop left a personal legacy, too. He and his wife Mary had six children, among them E.F. Benson, author of the *Mapp and Lucia* novels; A.C. Benson, who wrote the words of 'Land of Hope and Glory' to music by Elgar and became Master of Magdalene College, Oxford, and their archaeologist daughter, Margaret, who was the first woman to be granted a concession to excavate in Egypt.

Benson himself went on to be Archbishop of Canterbury before Truro Cathedral was completed, but in 1880, while it was being built and a temporary church was in use, he devised a special Christmas Eve service. He called it the Festival of Nine Lessons and Carols. King's College Chapel,

Photo: Tim Green

Cambridge adopted it and ever since it was first broadcast live from there in 1928, for many people, in Britain and around the world, this service is when Christmas really begins.

UNIVERSITY CHURCH OF ST MARY THE VIRGIN, OXFORD

Right on the High Street, surrounded by shops and university colleges, its spire one of the finest of all Oxford's 'dreaming spires', over the centuries the Parish Church of St Mary the Virgin has played a major role both in the development of the university and in an important movement in the Anglican Church. Enter through the porch on the High Street, but leave from the exit by the shop to view the exterior of the church in all its finery from Radcliffe Square.

It's hard to imagine now that a stone statue could have played a part in the beheading of an archbishop, but the Virgin and Child (still pockmarked by Parliamentarian bullet holes) and barley sugar columns around the entrance porch were cited as 'scandalous' during the trial of Archbishop Laud in 1641.

The elaborate porch had been built in 1637, just before the English Civil War, commissioned by the chaplain to William Laud, who was Archbishop of Canterbury, a close advisor to King Charles I and Chancellor of the University. His Puritan opponents, considering him much too 'Popish' and his ways a betrayal of the Protestant Reformation, found him guilty of high treason and had him executed on Tower Hill in London.

Almost a century earlier, in 1556, Thomas Cranmer, the

first Protestant Archbishop of Canterbury and responsible for the new Book of Common Prayer in English, was tried in St Mary's. One of the pillars in the nave is damaged, possibly during the erection of a platform for his trial.

This was during the reign of the Catholic Queen Mary, who hated Cranmer not only for his Protestantism but because he had been instrumental in her father, King Henry VIII's divorce from her mother, Queen Katharine of Aragon, and had officiated at the subsequent wedding to Anne Boleyn. He realised that recanting his beliefs would not save him, and he was burned at the stake in nearby Broad Street.

Thankfully, it's not all trial and tribulation in this appealing church, which has been an integral part of Oxford University since the 13th century when the scattered groups of scholars and tutors chose it as their central meeting place. They used it for academic lectures as well as Christian services, and for centuries the chapel – built by the then Rector, Adam de Brome, who founded Oriel College in 1324 – was used by the Chancellor of the University as a courtroom.

The nave and the chancel are in the late Perpendicular style, with slender columns and large, light-giving windows. If you go up into the gallery you get a good overall view of the church's interior and a close up on the great west window, depicting the Tree of Jesse surrounded by biblical figures. Look for the ceiling boss of Mahatma Gandhi, sitting cross-legged. It's in the north corner.

From the nave you can see how the chancel is aligned at a slight angle. Known as a 'weeping chancel' and popular in medieval churches, it symbolises the crucified Christ's head leaning towards the penitent thief.

The chancel is reserved for quiet prayer, the elm wood stalls are 15th century. Among the memorial tiles, one records the burial of Amy Robsart. She was the wife of

Photo: Tony Hisgett

Robert Dudley, a favourite of Queen Elizabeth I. She died in mysterious circumstances in 1560.

The large, ornately carved chair at the back of the nave is where the Chancellor sits, flanked by two Proctors, when attending university events. Look ahead to the 19th-century pulpit from where John Henry Newman, Vicar of St Mary's, called for a return to the orthodoxy of the early Church.

A renowned orator, he was one of the founders of the influential Oxford Movement, which sought to restore the Catholic tradition within the Church of England. Newman resigned as vicar in 1843, became a Roman Catholic and was made a cardinal in 1879. He was beatified in 2010.

In the south aisle, don't miss the splendid window by Augustus Pugin illustrating scenes from the life of St Thomas the Apostle, or the six white stone carvings along the wall. Known as Meditations on the Precious Blood they are based on original drawings by the Arts and Crafts artist Eric Gill for Westminster Cathedral (page 236).

Before Oxford University had buildings of its own, St Mary's was used as its administration centre, with a new building housing the first library, its books chained to desks. Now used as a parish room, it was here in 1942 that the Oxford Committee for Famine Relief was formed to consider ways to help people affected by the Second World War and its attendant food shortages, especially in Greece. It was the first meeting of what would later become the international relief agency, Oxfam.

Climb the tower's medieval spiral staircase for the best view of Oxford's skyline. The 127 winding stone steps pass the Old Library, the bell-ringing chamber and one of the oldest church clocks still in use, en route to the pinnacles, crockets, gargoyles and grotesques of the fine 13th-century steeple.

WELLS CATHEDRAL

Reached through ancient gateways, the Cathedral Church of St Andrew, Wells, stands, gracefully triumphant, in its field of green. Its great west front – 147 feet (45 metres) wide, as broad as it is high, dating from around 1230 – is a sculpture gallery. Beneath a modern Christ in Majesty are rows of figures, many life-sized, representing Bible stories and the Resurrection theme, and layer upon layer of prophets and patriarchs, saints, Apostles and angels. On a summer's evening, the creamy limestone setting for the largest gallery of medieval sculpture in the world turns warm and golden in the light of the setting sun.

Arguably the loveliest of the great English cathedrals, if the exterior is dramatic, the interior is a visual sensation. Your eye goes immediately to the pale, elegant strainer or 'scissor' arches at the nave crossing. Unique in English cathedrals, the simple yet stunning design looks modern, but in fact was an inspired 14th-century answer to the problem of a central bell tower unable to support the additional weight of a spire.

This is a much-used church, full of light and beauty. The pointed arches of the central nave are pleasingly proportioned while the simple vaulting reflecting the curve of the inverted (scissor) arches is delicately painted with an intricate Persian tree of life design.

Beautifully carved medieval capitals decorate columns in the aisles and transepts. Amid stylised foliage ('stiff-leaf') they picture moments in everyday life: a farmer chases a thieving fox, a cobbler hammers at a shoe, a man grimaces with toothache, boys steal grapes and get their come-uppance, a woman sews.

A passage and staircase in the south transept gives access to the library where the books date mainly from the 16th to the 18th centuries (earlier books and manuscripts were destroyed during the Reformation). Some are still chained to the book presses of 1686. Their subjects, ranging from theology to medicine, history, exploration and languages to science, reflect the interests of the clergy of that time.

In the north transept, look for the 24-hour astronomical clock which was installed around 1390. The outer circle of hours has twelve noon at the top, twelve midnight at the bottom; small gold stars mark the minutes in the second circle while the inner dial indicates the days of the month. A gold pointer shows the number of days since the New Moon. The clock's face displays the earth as the centre of the universe, the sun acts as the hour hand and on the quarter hour, jousting knights come out in tournament. Its medieval mechanism, replaced in 1837, is now in the Science Museum in London.

Windows bearing the cathedral's oldest stained glass, dating from around 1290, line a splendid staircase of well-worn steps that curves up to the octagonal chapter house.

Completed in 1306, it was where the business of the dean and canons (the chapter) was conducted. Ribs of the high vaulted roof radiate from a central pillar, fanning out to meet those flowing from the half columns placed at each corner of the octagon. Often compared to palm trees, the effect is of spacious elegance. Big windows are patterned with stone tracery but their original glass has mostly gone, smashed in the 17th century. Around the walls, nameplates indicate the canons' seating arrangements, a decorative pointed arch defining each stall. Stone-carved faces smile out from between the canopies.

The soaring, ornate quire has been at the heart of the

cathedral for over 800 years. Misericords hide beneath the wooden quire stalls. They date from the 1330s, each one carved from a single piece of oak, and depict animals, birds, humans and mythological figures set between two roundels of foliage. There's a cat chasing a mouse, a ewe feeding a lamb, a pair of parakeets in a pine tree and several figures appear to be doing what misericords do – supporting a seat.

Considered one of the most splendid examples of mid-14th-century stained glass, the great east window of the quire is often called the Golden Window for its glowing colours. It is a rare example of an intact Jesse Window of that period and shows Christ's family tree rising from Jesse, who was the father of King David. Being situated so high up probably saved it from destruction by the iconoclasts.

Wells was never a monastic foundation but does have cloisters, which were built over the first church that stood on this site back in 764. The stone-carved Saxon baptismal font survived and is in use in the cathedral.

Edging the peaceful lawns of Cathedral Green, picturesque Vicars' Close is a cul-de-sac of medieval houses and flower-filled gardens, built in 1348 to house the men of the choir. It is still home to members of the Vicars Choral.

Pass through the Penniless Porch and you are in the Market Place. William Penn, the founder of Pennsylvania, preached to a crowd of 3,000 souls here in 1685. Walking through the arched Bishop's Eye Gateway will lead you to the Bishop's Palace. In its splendid gardens are the wells that gave the town its name. Surrounded by high walls and a moat, entry is across a drawbridge complete with portcullis – and swans that summon food by pulling on a bell rope at the gatehouse.

Unlike most cities with a great cathedral, Wells is small. Sitting at the foot of Somerset's Mendip Hills, with peaceful

Photo: Michael D Beckwith

views out over sweeping fields, trees and green countryside, it still retains many of its ancient buildings.

WESTMINSTER CATHEDRAL

Built of red brick banded with contrasting white Portland stone, with its high Italianate campanile and crowning neo-Byzantine domes, Westminster Cathedral is a 20th-century landmark like no other. Approached across a wide piazza, set back from the soaring glass and steel of the revitalised area around Victoria Station, it is the seat of the Cardinal Archbishop of Westminster and the Mother Church for Roman Catholics in England and Wales.

If the exterior is impressive, the interior is spectacular – a vast space filled with marble and mosaics, eye-catching colour under dark and mysterious vaults.

For nearly 300 years until 1829, there were severe penalties for practising the Roman Catholic religion in Britain. In 1850, 21 years after Parliament passed the Roman Catholic Relief Act, Pope Pius IX restored the full Catholic hierarchy in England and established Catholic dioceses around the country.

Plans for a cathedral for Westminster came to fruition under the third archbishop, Cardinal Vaughan, on land purchased in Victoria, the site of the redundant Tothill Fields Prison.

Cardinal Vaughan was not about to compete with the matchless Gothic Westminster Abbey down the road or the Classic masterpiece that is St Paul's. He wanted a cathedral with a very large area for congregations and gatherings and favoured the Early Christian Byzantine style, influenced by the monumental Hagia Sophia in Constantinople, the mosaic-filled San Vitale in Ravenna and St Mark's in Venice.

His chosen architect for the project was John Francis Bentley and the foundation stone was laid in 1895. The fabric of the building was completed eight years later; the interior decoration is ongoing.

At the laying of the foundation stone, the cathedral was dedicated to The Most Precious Blood of Our Lord Jesus Christ, to his Blessed Mother, his Foster Father St Joseph and St Peter, his Vicar. To this were added secondary patrons: St Augustine and all British saints; St Patrick and all saints of Ireland. Not surprisingly, it is best known simply as Westminster Cathedral.

The statistics are astonishing: 12.5 million handmade bricks went into its construction and over 125 varieties of marble have been used in its decoration. Sourced from 24 countries on five continents, many of them were used in ancient Greece and Rome.

The dark green *verde antico* columns in the nave came from a quarry in Greece that supplied the columns for the Byzantine Hagia Sophia in 6th-century Constantinople. Their exquisite capitals, in Carrara marble from Tuscany, were individually designed in the Byzantine style. Each one took three months to complete by craftsmen working in pairs.

Mercifully uncluttered, Westminster has the highest and widest nave of all the English cathedrals, giving over 2,000 worshippers an unimpeded view of the high altar. A brightly-lit red crucifix, 30 feet (nine metres) tall and suspended between the nave and the sanctuary, seems to float out of the darkness of the cavernous domed vault overhead.

The high altar, a single block of unpolished Cornish granite, is framed by a lofty baldacchino (canopy) supported

Photo: Patche99z

by eight columns of yellow marble from Verona. Its gracefully arched white marble upper section is inlaid with lapis lazuli, pearl and gold. Inlays of coloured marble decorate the archbishop's throne, a smaller facsimile of that in the great basilica of St John Lateran in Rome.

In the sanctuary arch, a mosaic portrays Christ against a clear blue sky, with his feet on the earth and the Apostles lining up nearby. Hidden from view, the world-renowned choir sings from the apse behind the altar, giving an ethereal air to the beautiful music of the liturgy.

Eric Gill's famous fourteen Stations of the Cross are carried on the great piers of the nave. The controversial sculptor may have been virtually unknown when he was given the commission in 1914, but these stone-carved, highly stylised and complex narrative scenes are considered his finest work.

Beneath the thirteenth Station you'll find a precious treasure, an English alabaster statue of the Virgin and Child, carved in the Nottingham area around 1450. Shipped to France at the Reformation, it was discovered in Paris in 1955 and enshrined here as Our Lady of Westminster.

A circuit of ornate, richly decorated chapels edges the nave, each one an individual, each one with a story to tell, all filled with glittering, mesmerising mosaics.

Cardinal Vaughan wanted the chapels to portray the Christian journey from life to death, starting with the Baptistry (on the right as you enter the cathedral) and ending with the Chapel of the Holy Souls (on the left).

Next to the Baptistry, with its huge octagonal font reminiscent of those used in early Christian basilicas, particularly San Vitale in Ravenna, is the chapel dedicated to St Gregory and St Augustine. Mosaics tell the story of the evangelisation of England and its early saints. Next door, the suitably green Chapel of St Patrick and the Saints of Ireland has Celtic designs inlaid on the floor and remembers the 50,000 Irishmen who died in the First World War.

The Chapel of St Andrew and the Saints of Scotland is a magnificent mix of the Byzantine style of art (St Andrew is also the patron saint of Greece) and exquisite furnishings by leaders of the Arts and Crafts Movement. With a particularly fine mosaic pavement, the Chapel of St Paul tells of his conversion and travels.

Across the nave in the north aisle, there are chapels dedicated to St Joseph and to St George and the English Martyrs, which has Eric Gill's last carving above the altar. It also has the chair and kneeler made for Queen Elizabeth II in 1995 when she attended Choral Vespers during the cathedral's centenary celebrations – the first visit by a reigning sovereign to a Roman Catholic service in England since the Reformation.

Finally there's the Holy Souls Chapel. John Francis Bentley died in 1902 while the cathedral was still being built and this is the only chapel in which every detail is to the design of the architect himself. Amid gleaming gold, the 'old' Adam is shown by the forbidden tree, with the 'new' Adam the Risen Christ, and on one wall, a powerful image of purgatory.

With every surface centimetre covered in marble and patterned in light-catching mosaics, the Lady Chapel, to the right of the high altar, is a glowing masterpiece. It offers a glimpse into Bentley's vision for the entire cathedral when it is completed.

There is so much to see here, so much colour and detail to take in, that one visit is never enough. And then there are the spectacular views across London from the towering campanile to consider. No medieval winding stairs to negotiate here, a lift will deliver you to the viewing gallery 210 feet (64 metres) above street level.

WHITBY ABBEY

High on its headland, a landmark from land and sea, the dark outline of Whitby's Abbey Church looms over the hillside town and its harbour. It's the archetypal Gothic ruin.

A defining moment in the history of the Christian Church took place here in AD 664 at the Synod of Whitby.

At that time there were two strands of the religion. One came via St Augustine, sent by Pope Gregory I (The Great) from Rome, who landed in Kent in 597 and converted the pagan king and his people to the Christian faith. Among his followers was Paulinus. He reached Northumbria in 627, converted King Edwin and baptised his household.

The other came with the Celtic missionaries from Iona. After converting the inhabitants of Scotland they moved south into Northumbria, making Lindisfarne their chief mission centre in the 630s. Relatively isolated, they had little contact with Rome.

While both were spreading the Christian faith among the people of Northumbria, the two had some different traditions, crucially in the way that the date of Easter was calculated. This caused much confusion.

The Synod of Whitby solved this once and for all, coming down on the side of Rome. Its point had been put strongly by Wilfrid, Abbot of Ripon, whose argument that Rome's authority came directly from St Peter, who held the keys to the kingdom of heaven, won the day. The date when Easter falls each year has been calculated in the same way ever since.

The Synod took place at the monastery founded in 657 by the remarkable abbess, St Hild (also known as Hilda). Housing both monks and nuns, it was one of the most important religious centres in the Anglo-Saxon world. The burial place of the kings of Northumbria, five of its monks became bishops, and it was home to Caedmon, the first named English poet.

Viking raids in the mid- to late 9th century probably put an end to Hild's abbey and community up on the headland known then as Streaneshalch. The name 'Whitby' is Danish and the town around the harbour is likely to have been founded by Danish settlers in the 10th century.

That a great new abbey rose on the site in the 11th century is down to a Norman soldier, Reinfrid, a companion of William the Conqueror at the Battle of Hastings. He came across the abbey ruins in the wild landscape amid sea and sky and was so moved that he took holy orders and returned to live there. By 1078 he had founded a small priory of monks, which over time became a large Benedictine monastery.

The outline of part of its church, built in the Romanesque style around 1109, has been marked out in the grass of Whitby Abbey's dramatic ruins.

Bishop Roger of Scarborough is likely to have ordered the rebuilding of Whitby Abbey, dedicated to St Peter and St Hild, around the 1220s, a time when lavish and ambitious rebuilding projects were taking place all over England. Its style is English Gothic and the transepts are similar to those of York Minster (page 258).

The presbytery, seven bays long and the site of the quire and high altar, still stands to its original height. Except for the south aisle wall, its shell is more or less complete. Richly moulded pointed arches rise from clustered columns. Above

Photo: Mdbeckwith

is the triforium, an arcaded gallery, and above that the clerestory with a single-light window in each bay. Elaborate stone carvings give some intimation of how grand it all was in its day.

Although there's little documentary evidence, the different styles of architecture found in the building suggest that it took about 250 years to complete the church.

Approached from the town below via 199 steep and winding stone steps – or the easy route, from the car park – the most impressive facade is that of the eastern wall of the presbytery. The west front had been equally impressive, but much of it collapsed in the late 18th century and further damage was inflicted in 1914, when German Navy ships shelled Whitby.

The Abbey may stand in splendid isolation today, but there's evidence that people lived on the headland in Roman times, even during the Bronze Age, thus well before the thriving Anglian community of the 7th to 9th centuries. (The term 'Anglian' is used to distinguish the Angles, people who settled in the north and along the east coast in the 5th and 6th centuries, from the Saxons who settled in the south and west of England.)

Shortly after 1539, when the Abbey was suppressed during the dissolution of the monasteries, the wealthy Cholmeley family acquired its estates. They demolished all the monastic buildings except the abbot's lodging, which they used as a house mainly in the summer (and which generations of Cholmeleys remodelled).

What was left of the church after the king's commissioners had stripped it, but still an impressive if empty shell, remained to stand untouched. Battered and weakened by the elements, large parts of it collapsed over succeeding centuries. Its ruins inspired Bram Stoker's Gothic tale of *Dracula*.

Now in the care of English Heritage, the visitor centre in the former Cholmeley House displays finds from all periods of the abbey's history together with computer-generated images and interactive touchscreens. A £1.6 million transformation of Whitby Abbey in 2019 has resulted in new displays and better facilities for visitors.

Just down the headland from the abbey ruins, at the top of those infamous 199 steps, is Whitby's parish church. St Mary's was built by the abbey for the townspeople, probably in the early 12th century, though why so high and so far from the town below is not known. It is certainly in a spectacular site and well worth visiting for its extraordinary Georgian interior, filled with 17th- and 18th-century box pews and complex galleries.

WINCHESTER CATHEDRAL

With the longest medieval nave in Europe and architecture that spans all the main styles of English church building from the 11th to the early 16th centuries, Winchester's massive Cathedral Church of the Holy Trinity, St Peter, St Paul and St Swithun is a history lesson in stone.

Before its construction began in 1079 under the conquering Normans, there was a Saxon cathedral and Benedictine monastery here, founded by Alfred the Great. Known as the 'Old Minster', its diocese stretched from the English Channel to the River Thames.

At the time, Winchester was the capital of Saxon England and centre of power. Here kings were crowned and buried. It is said that on 15 July in 971, when the bones of the saintly

bishop, Swithun, were translated into the minster from the cemetery outside, where he'd asked to be buried, such was his resentment that the heavens opened and it didn't stop raining for 40 days. St Swithun's Day has gone down into the annals of British summer weather forecasting.

Given such an important site, when Bishop Walkelyn arrived in 1070 he planned his new cathedral to be the biggest and the best of all the post-Conquest cathedrals. You can still see some of his vision in the northern transept: towering, powerful and sturdy, its rounded arches unadorned. Also in the low-vaulted crypt, which frequently floods, a reminder that he took little notice of the marshy ground on which he was building.

Over the next five centuries, a succession of bishops made their mark, adding and remodelling in the architectural styles that were fashionable in their day.

The spectacular nave was predominantly the work of Bishop William of Wykeham, the most powerful statesman and reputedly the richest man in late 14th-century England, despite his humble origins. Twice Chancellor of England, he founded New College Oxford and then Winchester College public school, its alumni known to this day as Wykehamists.

The architect, William Wynford, used the Norman three-tiered walls as a base and re-clad them in the latest Perpendicular Gothic style. The result is a stupendous creamy white avenue of tall, slender pillars and pointed arches, all towering heavenwards to an exotic canopy forested with palm tree fronds. It's a view guaranteed to stop you in your tracks.

Unusually, the great west window is a mosaic of stained glass. It was created from fragments found all over the building after the destruction wrought by Oliver Cromwell's forces during the English Civil War of the 1640s.

Crowds gather around the grave of Jane Austen, who is buried in the north aisle. The stone in the floor makes no mention of her literary skills, but her nephew's brass plaque and a later memorial window funded by public subscription try to make up for that.

Nearby is a 12th-century font, still in use. In black Tournai marble, the sides are carved with birds and scenes from the life and miracles of St Nicholas, patron saint of children. Probably given to the cathedral by William the Conqueror's wealthy grandson, Henry of Blois, who was a Bishop of Winchester, it was used to baptise the infant King Henry III.

Fabulous wealth and enormous power went hand-in-hand for many of Winchester's bishops, who counted among their number eleven Chancellors of England. They had a splendid palace in Southwark and a grand priory church, St Mary Overie (now Southwark Cathedral, page 209) from where they ran the country.

Several had chantry chapels of majestic proportions built at Winchester so the monks could 'chant' daily prayers there for the peaceful repose of their souls. Built between the 14th and 16th centuries, each one is an exquisite example of the stonemasons' art.

Four of these chapels are set in the retroquire near the high altar, but Bishop William of Wykeham's is in the nave's south aisle. His effigy lies in prayerful pose under towering gables, richly clothed and clutching his crozier, attended at his head by worried looking angels. Three secretaries sit poised at his feet. It wasn't desecrated during the Cromwellian rampage because, it is said, the soldier charged with shattering it had been educated at Winchester College and wouldn't despoil the founder's tomb.

In the north transept, the small Epiphany Chapel has richly coloured stained-glass windows by the Pre-Raphaelite artist Edward Burne-Jones. In contrast, the nearby Holy Sepulchre Chapel displays remarkable wall paintings from the 1170s of Christ being taken down from the cross and placed in his tomb. A reminder of how the Norman cathedral would have looked, they were discovered during renovations in the 1960s.

This transept also has steps down into the crypt where Antony Gormley's enigmatic life-sized sculpture, 'Sound II', contemplates the water held in his cupped hands. In the rainy months when the crypt floods, it can be almost up to its knees in water.

The south transept is home to 'Kings and Scribes: The Birth of a Nation'. An innovative permanent exhibition on three levels, it explores the text and illuminated pages of the four-volume Winchester Bible, reveals manuscripts from the cathedral's archives and tells the story of how Winchester was founded on the power of saints and kings. The 12th-century Winchester Bible is one of the finest examples of medieval art still in existence. Just one scribe wrote its entire text in Latin on the skins of 250 calves, a task that lasted about four years.

Between the transepts, the enclosed presbytery and quire is another breathtaking space. The intricately carved quire stalls with their gabled canopies are of oak, made in the 1300s. As the carvings only depicted animals, human faces, foliage and mythical beasts they were not destroyed at the Reformation. High above, the restored vault is studded with 107 fine roof bosses.

The great screen (reredos) behind the altar, with the crucified Christ at its centre, was completed in 1475 and covered in brightly coloured statues of saints. These were removed during the Reformation. That the screen looks immaculate today is due to the Gothic Revival architect Sir George Gilbert Scott, who replicated them and added representatives of the English church. These include Edward the Confessor who was crowned in the Old Minster, the hymn writer John Keble who was a local vicar, and a small statue of Queen Victoria.

Perched atop the presbytery screens are mortuary chests containing the bones of early Saxon kings, including those of Cnut and his wife, Emma. When the Parliamentarians raided the cathedral they threw the bones out and scattered them around. They were later returned to the caskets, in no particular order.

The massive Early English Gothic retroquire, built to accommodate the pilgrims who flocked to the shrine of St Swithun, is packed with magnificent chapels.

Angels peer down from the ceiling of the suitably named Guardian Angels Chapel. Dating from the 1200s, they were painted by the royal painter, Master William. Dedicated to the Virgin Mary, the large Lady Chapel has a Jesse Window showing Christ's ancestry and wall paintings of events in Mary's life. They are good copies of originals from the 1500s. The restored vault in the Langton Chapel is a reminder of the vibrant colours that would once have adorned the cathedral. Here, too, are the ornate chantry chapels of four fabulously wealthy Bishops of Winchester.

Among the many memorials is the portrait bronze of a 20th-century hero, deep-sea diver William Walker, who 'with his own two hands saved the cathedral'. For six years from 1906, Walker worked for six hours a day in total darkness, in the thick and murky underground water that was causing the building to sink, laying 25,000 bags of concrete to create a solid base for the subsiding walls to then be underpinned by a team of 150 bricklayers.

A stone screen at the back of the high altar's reredos was the site of St Swithun's shrine. Pilgrims would have crawled through its tunnel, known as the 'holy hole', to be close to the saint's relics. For 400 years these were displayed on the altar in a reliquary containing more than 300 pounds (140 kilograms) of silver, rubies and gold. Naturally that disappeared at the Reformation.

The nine gabled niches in the screen that originally held statues of saints are now filled with superb icons created by Sergei Fyodorov in the 1990s. Before it stands a canopied memorial hearse, made to mark the 1,100th anniversary of St Swithun's death. Look down. The tiles you are walking on are medieval.

The peaceful Inner Close with its gardens and fine buildings are a grand place to wander. John Keats wrote his 'Season of mist and mellow fruitfulness' ode to autumn while he was staying in Winchester, inspired by his daily walk past the cathedral and college and through the water meadows.

A Keats Trail will take you through the Cathedral's Inner Close with its 14th-century Deanery and half-timbered Cheney Court, past Jane Austen's last home on College Street, where she wrote *Persuasion*, then on to Bishop Wykeham's magnificent Winchester College and the water meadows beyond. It makes the perfect ending to an inspiring day.

WORCESTER CATHEDRAL

Standing majestically above the River Severn, the Cathedral Church of Christ and the Blessed Mary the Virgin of Worcester reflects every period in England's turbulent history. If you are fortunate enough to visit when the organ is being played, you may feel that the whole building seems to soar and sing.

Nothing survives of the first cathedral here, built in 680 and dedicated to Saints Peter and Paul. However, stone from the 10th-century Saxon cathedral, founded by St Oswald around 966 and dedicated to St Mary, was used in the present building. This was begun by Bishop Wulfstan in 1084 and his legacy is one of the finest crypts to be found among medieval cathedrals.

When St Oswald's cathedral was being demolished to make way for the new Norman construction, St Wulfstan is said to have wept: 'We have destroyed the work of saints, we neglect our souls so we can pile up stones.' In 1089 he had the shrine of St Oswald translated into the completed eastern part of the new cathedral.

He must have been both a charismatic man of God and a shrewd politician for he served as Bishop of Worcester under two Anglo-Saxon kings and two Norman kings. On his death in 1095, he was immediately venerated as a saint by local people, although he was not formally canonised until 1203.

Wulfstan made an oath of fealty to the new Norman rulers while quietly encouraging his monks to keep up the Anglo-Saxon traditions of writing their chronicle and biographies of recent bishops and saints in English. Today's cathedral library is grateful for that.

Built from a blend of golden Cotswold limestone and green sandstone from Shropshire, his cathedral was huge by Saxon standards, almost the size it is now. There's a model in the crypt of how it probably looked at the time.

At first sight on entering the cathedral the long nave appears to be of a single design, but in fact it was rebuilt in different styles over a period of 200 years. A closer look reveals the two westernmost bays of 1175 have the Transitional Norman/Gothic mix of slightly pointed arches while the rest of the nave, which dates from the 14th century, soars on the slim columns and pointed arches of the Decorated and then the Perpendicular Gothic styles.

It was only after the western bays were completed that the cathedral was formally consecrated. This took place in 1218, in the presence of King Henry III and an illustrious company of bishops and abbots, and St Wulfstan got a new shrine near the high altar. Just two years earlier, Henry's father, King John, had been buried here.

The great west window, with its eight slim lancets rising to a fine multi-petalled rose, is filled with excellent 19th-century, neo-medieval stained glass that depicts the creation of the world and the Garden of Eden (search for the pink giraffe). The biblical story continues with the life of Christ, the 'new Adam', at the far end of the cathedral in the great east window.

The west end of the building contains many memorials, particularly statues of former Bishops of Winchester. A window to look for commemorates the composer Sir Edward Elgar, who lived much of his life in and around the city. It depicts 'The Dream of Gerontius', one of his greatest works.

Elgar conducted the first performance of his revised version of the 'Enigma Variations' (the one that's usually heard) at the Three Choirs Festival held in Worcester in 1899. The oldest music festival in the world, it takes place every year at the end of July, rotating between the cathedrals of Worcester, Gloucester (page 88) and Hereford (page 101), their choirs being central to the programme.

At the crossing you can look up into the base of the cathedral's 14th-century tower, one of England's finest. King Charles II watched the Battle of Worcester unravel from up there in 1651.

From here to the east end is very much a story of Victorian restoration under the hand of the 19th-century Gothic

Revival architect, Sir Giles Gilbert Scott. He also designed the flamboyant pulpit, heavily carved in marble and alabaster, and the nave's flooring, strikingly patterned in Sicilian white and Kilkenny black marble.

Steps from the crossing lead up to the quire through Scott's ornate screen, a fine piece of metalwork worth a close look for the detail of saints and trumpeting angels.

With its graceful stone arches and delicately painted ceiling, the quire is splendid. The quire stalls may be Victorian but 39 of the 42 misericords beneath the seats date from 1379 and include almost a complete cycle of Labours of the Months. Their subjects range from biblical stories to the weird and wonderful, all depicted in great detail. Here are men haymaking, a swineherd collecting acorns and 'the clever daughter', a woman, naked under a net, riding a goat with a rabbit under her arm.

The grand tomb of King John stands before the steps up to the high altar. The despised King, who had visited Worcester and stayed at the priory on several occasions, had a special devotion to St Wulfstan. During the civil war at the end of John's reign, Worcester sided with the rebellious barons. For this the city was fined 200 marks and the shrine of St Wulfstan was melted down in order to pay it, which angered the King greatly.

Despite this, when he was lying mortally ill in Newark in 1216, still feuding with his barons, he requested to be buried in the cathedral between St Wulfstan and St Oswald. On his tomb effigy, miniatures of both saints are positioned at his head. Dating from 1232, it is the oldest royal effigy in England. The carved marble base was made in 1529.

To the right of the altar is Prince Arthur's elaborate chantry chapel. He died at Ludlow in 1502, only a few months after his marriage to Katharine of Aragon, aged just fifteen.

Photo: Sonofdenn62

His magnificent funeral, which his parents King Henry VII and Elizabeth of York were too grieved to attend, was said to include a knight in armour riding the prince's horse up the nave and into the quire.

The chapel for 'the king we never had' took twelve years to complete. It is covered with stone-carved figures of kings and saints and an array of Tudor heraldry and symbols, together with Katharine's emblem, the pomegranate.

The east end was rebuilt over the Norman crypt in the 13th century. It is in the Early English Gothic style with some of the Purbeck Marble shafts soaring to a height of 65 feet (almost twenty metres).

This was the work of Bishop William of Blois, who replaced the original semi-circular building with a rectangular one, adding two small transepts and three chapels, the Lady Chapel being in the centre.

It not only lengthened the cathedral considerably, giving it a new sense of space, height and light, but extended the space available for the pilgrims who came in large numbers to the shrines of St Oswald and St Wulfstan. In the Middle Ages the devotion to the Virgin Mary was so great that the Lady Chapel attracted even more pilgrims.

At the Reformation the shrines were dismantled and, according to the chronicle, the bones of the saints were wrapped in lead and buried to the north of the high altar. They've never been found, so presumably they are still there.

The surrender of the cathedral monastery took place in January 1540. A year later, King Henry VIII signed new statutes that handed the government of the cathedral to a dean and chapter of canons.

During the English Civil War of 1642 to 1651, Worcester was unwavering in its support of the King and so became harshly fought over. The cathedral suffered badly when the

Parliamentarians broke in and wrought devastation. The nave and cloisters were used to house the troops and their horses, the aisles used as latrines.

The crypt, reached by steps in the south transept, is one of the loveliest in England. The most complete part of St Wulfstan's Norman cathedral, it's a quiet world of gently curving arches and simple stone pillars, some possibly from the old Saxon cathedral. Storyboards in its aisle tell the cathedral's history.

Outside, the cloisters date from the late 14th and early 15th centuries and were restored in the 19th, when the tracery in the windows was added. In warm red sandstone with lierne vaulting above, it has lavish windows dividing the monks' study carrels, looking out onto the garden (garth). Their washbasins can be seen in the west walk. In the centre bay of the south cloister, the etched Millennium Window commemorates the Christian life of the city, county and diocese through the past thousand years.

The cloisters connected the main buildings of the monastery, including the splendid chapter house to the east, where the monks met every day. Planned by St Wulfstan and built around 1100, its interior is circular, the first of its kind.

The ribs of the vault seem to flow out like a fountain from a central column and the continuous arcaded seating around the walls ensured that no monk was considered more important than another. The acoustics are such that one person speaking could be heard by all, wherever they were seated.

College Green on the south side of the cathedral marks the outer precinct of the monastery and contains the ruins of the 'Guesten hall' where pilgrims and guests were received. The Edgar Tower, built in the mid-14th century, is still the main entrance to the Cathedral precincts from the city. On the other side of College Green, the Watergate leads out to the riverside walk from where there are good views back to Worcester's stately cathedral.

YORK MINSTER

Vast, Gothic and boasting the biggest expanse of medieval glass in the world, the largest chapter house and some of the finest windows in England, the Cathedral Church of St Peter in York (better known as York Minster), seat of England's second archbishop, isn't short on superlatives.

Its story goes back to a little wooden church hurriedly erected in 627 for the baptism of Edwin, King of Northumbria. He wished to wed the Christian princess Ethelburga of Kent and his conversion was a condition of the marriage. That church, rebuilt in stone and dedicated to St Peter, burned down; as did the next one. Invading Danes demolished the third church and it was only in 1080 that the north was sufficiently settled for the Norman Archbishop of York, Thomas of Bayeux, to begin work on rebuilding the Minster.

By the 13th century, however, its style of architecture was looking decidedly old fashioned and not considered impressive enough for the important city of York. The scale of the new Minster, finally dedicated in 1472, transformed it into the biggest medieval cathedral in England.

The exuberant west front has vast pinnacled towers; the great 15th-century tower rises in majestic simplicity. For all its size, the Minster's interior is surprisingly delicate and uncluttered, the awe-inspiring nave lit by immense windows. The nave's wooden vault, painted to look like stone, has bosses showing the life of Christ. They are Victorian replicas, replaced after one of the many fires that have dogged the building's history, but it's difficult to tell they are not originals.

York's stained glass is legendary. The west window, its heart-shaped centre created by glorious tracery and known as 'the Heart of Yorkshire' is stunning. Archbishops, saints and the principal events in the life of Christ range across its eight slender lancets, topped by the depiction of the Coronation of the Virgin and Christ in Majesty. It looks impressive from close up, but walk down the nave and look back to get the full impact.

Dominating the Lady Chapel, the east window, created nearly 70 years later in 1405, appears like a giant curtain of brilliance set in tiers of fine tracery. At over 76 feet (23 metres) high, it contains the largest single expanse of medieval stained glass in the world and amid angels, saints and martyrs it combines stories from the Book of Genesis in the Old Testament and the Book of Revelation – the beginning and the end.

In the north transept, Early Gothic in style, the Five Sisters Window dates from around 1260 and is the oldest complete window in the Minster. At 53 feet (sixteen metres), it is one of the tallest in England, and is composed of over 100,000 tiny panes dotted with colour. Look for the panel at the bottom depicting Daniel in the lion's den. It is Norman in origin and predates the window by a century at least.

The window was removed during the First World War to protect it from Zeppelin raids. When it was restored in the 1920s it was rededicated to the women of the British Empire who lost their lives in that war, the only such memorial in the country.

Nearby, an astronomical clock depicts the position of the sun and stars from the viewpoint of a pilot flying over York.

Photo: Jitka Erbenová

Installed in 1955, it is dedicated to the aircrews who flew from nearby airfields during the Second World War and were killed in action.

High up in the south transept, the rose window is a remarkable survivor of the devastating fire of July 1984. The 7,000 pieces of glass were cracked in about 40,000 places, yet the window remained in one piece. The rescue work took three years to complete.

While the stonework that supports it is 13th century, the glass is a mix from the 16th, 18th and 20th centuries and includes red and white roses honouring the union of the Houses of Lancaster and York (Henry VII's marriage to Elizabeth of York in 1486) that ended the Wars of the Roses.

That the Minster's magnificent medieval glass survived the English Civil War was down to Yorkshireman Thomas Fairfax. When in 1644, York fell to Oliver Cromwell's forces after the decisive Battle of Marston Moor, the city was surrendered to the Parliamentarian commander on the condition that the cathedral wasn't damaged. Fairfax kept his promise. Today more than half of all the medieval glass in England is found here.

The 1984 fire destroyed the south transept roof with just six of the 68 vaulting bosses surviving the blaze. New ones were carved, including some designed by children to reflect 20th-century achievements and concerns. These include the moon landing, space exploration, a starving African child and saving the whale.

At the central crossing, gaze up to view the light and airy view of the tower vault and then take a look at the gilded detail on the pulpitum. Known as the King's Screen for its carved statues of kings of England from William the Conqueror to Henry VI, that there are fifteen of them means the doorway into the quire is off-centre. There's a theory that the screen was designed in 1420 to hold fourteen statues, but the early demise of Henry V in 1422, before the screen was finished, made the hasty inclusion of Henry VI necessary.

Linked by a vestibule from the north transept, the octagonal chapter house is a masterpiece of construction. It has no central column – the ceiling is supported by timbers in the roof, an engineering technique that was revolutionary in the 13th century. Much of its 14th-century glass survives. Rising up to meet the vaulted roof, these beautiful big windows with their subtle geometric tracery flood the building with light. In the stone walls and canopies, strange beasts hide and myriad faces peep out from among beautifully carved foliage.

NOTES

NOTES

NOTES